ENERGY PLAN FOR THE WESTERN MAN

JOSEPH BEUYS IN AMERICA

WRITINGS BY AND INTERVIEWS WITH THE ARTIST

COMPILED BY CARIN KUONI

FOUR WALLS EIGHT WINDOWS
NEW YORK

Writings by Joseph Beuys included herein © 1990
The Estate of Joseph Beuys

Selection and "Editor's Note" ©1990 Carin Kuoni
Introduction © 1990 Kim Levin
"Beuys in America..." © 1990 Caroline Tisdall

Published by:
Four Walls Eight Windows
PO Box 548, Village Station
New York, N.Y., 10014

U.K. offices:
Four Walls Eight Windows/Turnaround
27 Horsell Road, London, N51 XL England

First paperback edition. First printing August 1993.

Library of Congress Cataloging-in-Publication Data:
Joseph Beuys in America: Energy plan for the Western Man. Writings
by and Interviews with the Artist.—1st ed.
p.   cm.
1. Beuys, Joseph—Political and social views. 2. Beuys, Joseph—
Aesthetics.
I. Title.
N6888.B463A35   1990
700'.1—dc 20   90-37433
                                            CIP

ISBN: 1-56858-007-X

Text design by Cindy LaBreacht.
Printed in the United States.

ENERGY PLAN FOR THE WESTERN MAN

JOSEPH BEUYS
IN AMERICA

Table of Contents

v

vi   *Contents*

ACKNOWLEDGEMENT

At the origin of this book are Eva Beuys and Bernd Klüser. They not only made it possible with important advice but shaped it substantially. I am grateful to them for their patient and sensitive collaboration.

Ronald Feldman and Caroline Tisdall, together with Thomas M. Messer, initiated Joseph Beuys' contacts with the United States—eventually on the very inclusive, grand and historic scale of the Guggenheim Museum retrospective in 1979/1980. Ronald Feldman also provided me with the first, and therefore the most decisive, support. I thank him for his advice and the use of the archives of Ronald Feldman Fine Arts. Caroline Tisdall quietly offered me insightful guidance from the beginning. I am grateful to her for many ideas and for her essay in which she brings together the important aspects of Joseph Beuys' work; at the same time the artist's view of this new—American—cultural sphere is re-evoked. Kim Levin complements this account from the artist's perspective with an essay that addresses the impact of Joseph Beuys' work on the American art scene. I thank her for this valuable contribution.

The texts are supplemented with a few photographs for which I would like to thank Eva Beuys, Caroline Tisdall, Sarah Lees from the Dia Art Foundation in New York, and Sigrun Paas from the Hessischen Landesmuseum in Darmstadt.

Arne Svenson helped at the last minute with friendship and professionalism. John Oakes, my editor, was again the source of my inspiration.

—CARIN KUONI

EDITOR'S NOTE

Carin Kuoni

When Joseph Beuys finally visited the United States, he enacted a performance piece called "Energy Plan for the Western Man." He elaborated on this "plan" during a month-long trip at the beginning of 1974 that took him to New York, Chicago and Minneapolis. The plan consisted of no precise solutions or advice but was itself the continuous, physical and spiritual interaction between the artist and his audience. The enlargement of communicative means and a widened understanding of world-shaping powers constituted for Beuys the true source of human empowerment; to him the exchanges between audience and artist were a source of constant metamorphosis, a state of mind that was, however, bound to and shaped by the specific moment and the specific place. These historically fixed encounters would remain as energy sources: they would function as a battery of sorts. The idea of an energy pool, or battery, surfaces often in his work. That Joseph Beuys brought to Western Man something that one would assume to be inherent to Western Man—the energy plan of the Western Man—reveals Joseph Beuys' understanding of the purpose of this trip as a healing act in which differing assumptions would be brought to a synthesis.

Joseph Beuys aimed at recreating an all encompassing unity between material and spiritual, human, animal and vegetative realms. This wholeness alone—and not its extreme and singular coordinates—would in his opinion assure the survival for mankind in the fullest and most creative freedom. As much as his work is suggestive of this unity, it also deals with this unity's absence. From this approach come such works as his "dialogue" with the coyote in New York in 1974 and his concentration on an "Energy Plan for Western Man," so clearly evoking the notion of Eastern Man.

Beuys returned to the United States only a few times. Ronald Feldman had made his first appearance in this country possible by agreeing to present as Beuys' first American exhibition no tangible works: that is, an empty room. Instead Beuys travelled, lecturing and listening, through America. The artist later remarked—half in jest—that his retrospective at the Guggenheim Museum, the largest museum exhibition during his lifetime, had cost him half a year of his creative life. As he grew older, Beuys placed more and more emphasis on his live appearances, lectures, public discussions and interviews and less on art objects.

This book presents Joseph Beuys' thoughts and ideas in the words with which he chose to address his American audience. They reveal not only the often light-hearted spirit at such gatherings but show the artist in his struggle to approach a new audience of which he had certain preconceptions. In this respect these texts are not just about Joseph Beuys in America but about a single man interacting with a myriad of human ideas, trying to shape and unite other men in an elementary humanism.

The texts and interviews assembled in this book either appeared in English-language art magazines or were written or given in English by the artist. A few additional texts by the artist are included to present Joseph Beuys from a wider perspective than that of his American trip and to provide some of his most elemental thoughts to further the reader's understanding of the other texts.

The headlines under which the texts have been gathered in three chapters—"Social Sculpture," "Its Elements," "The Site"— may serve as probes with which to examine the immense fund of thought that Beuys opened in each of his appearances. The Social Sculpture—just as the language-oriented Energy Plan— for Joseph Beuys is the essentially immaterial act of shaping creative ideas and freeing creative energies. The reader may witness some Social Sculpture in the first chapter of the book. The tangible traces or elements of these "laboratories," the documents of these actions, are discussed with references to specific works in the second chapter. Finally, the texts in the third chapter are a testimony to the scope of Beuys' vision, that knew neither geographical nor material boundaries. As his approach aimed at synthesis, the division of his work into chapters must be, to some degree, arbitrary.

Because publication of the few English texts by Joseph Beuys has been irregularly scattered over the last twenty years, a chronological presentation of the development of his vision could not be attempted. In presenting the interviews in their original length I tried to preserve in these texts the frailty of human speech. This brings these treatises to life at the same time as it reveals them locked in a historic time frame distant from the reader's. But Joseph Beuys' profoundly human search for meaning will reach any reader, even through the veil of history.

Introduction

KIM LEVIN

"In the late 1960s, Joseph Beuys was an underground name in the American art world, and a hero to art students. His reputation preceded him to the United States. When we heard of his use of fat and felt, we thought of our own postminimal involvements at the time in nonart materials and informal structure. When we saw bits and pieces of his work—a felt suit, a silver broom, a blackboard with scrawls—we related it to Oldenburg, to Pop Art. When he came to New York in 1974 and talked to a coyote in a gallery, we interpreted it in terms of our own performance art. The parallels were misleading. In our literal climate, we never suspected that he was a symbolist, an expressionist, a mystical romanticist," I wrote in 1980. "Although rumors of his activities were reaching us in the Sixties, and his actions—incompletely understood—may have instigated some of our own, Beuys was speaking to a different culture, was coming from a different past.

We may have made use of his eccentric materiality, but we never knew his intentions."

On his first tour of the U.S.A. in 1974, Beuys himself was preceded by newspaper accounts describing him as "the Picasso of the avant-garde." Since Picasso at that time was out of favor and the avant-garde was loudly said to be dead, this was a double-edged compliment. Beuys and his work were greeted in America with derision, suspicion, and distaste, as well as fascination and awe. First U.S. tour? Since when did artists make grand tours—thirty meetings in ten days—that radiated constant media attention? Beuys carried the modernist stance to its inevitable conclusion: he displaced the "aura" (that Walter Benjamin had thought lost) from artwork to artist.

How did America react to Joseph Beuys? With misunderstandings, of course. It wasn't widely known here, until 1979–80 when he turned his retrospective at the Guggenheim Museum into a spiralling progression of "Stations" (of the cross, of the trains to concentration camps) that Beuys' work contained a secret narrative, that it was religious, social, political, historical—referring to the specifics of the Third Reich—and meant to be therapeutic as well as symbolically autobiographical. It was our mistake.

The major Beuys exhibition at the Guggenheim more than corrected that. Since then, in fact, his intentions may have overshadowed his art. His words, his deeds, his teachings, his theories of Social Sculpture, his persona, and his indelible image have permeated our understanding of his work. There's no need to go into the authorized version of the legend—which was, as are all parthenogenic myths of unique creation, in the end as limiting as it was protective—or into the attempts to question it. The cult of personality that surrounded Beuys was nearly impenetrable. He tried to exercise total control. The number of books on Beuys' life and art that never saw the light of day is legion. Who knows what they would have told us?

So, though we've learned a great deal in the past decade about his intentions, we know less about the discrepancies in his work between intention and result, which, as Duchamp once pointed out, is where the "art quotient" happens. And we know little yet about the influences and relationships that may be the bane of individualistic artists but are the stuff of art history.

Beuys' convoluted iconography of personal ritual and Germanic symbolism left no room for influences. The messiah stance required that his early Fluxus connections be played down and his uniqueness played up. Perhaps we heard at some point that he broke off with George Maciunas, the founder of Fluxus, but few people here realized that Beuys had helped organize a Fluxus concert in Düsseldorf in 1963, or that he was in a Nam June Paik performance in 1964. We knew about the disagreement Beuys had with Marcel Broodthaers, who was in the beginning a member of the Organization for Direct Democracy, and who publically accused Beuys of Wagnerism. But no one told us about the influence on Beuys of Yves Klein, who came to Krefeld and Düsseldorf at the start of the Sixties with his Blue Revolution, and with whom Beuys exhibited and made public dialogues.

And who in America could possibly have known that the work of Henry Dunant—the founder of the Red Cross and a visionary artist—had a major impact on Beuys's vision of the function of art. In Europe, as well as in America, this has gone unremarked and remains to be explored. Did Dunant's "fire piano" lead to Beuys's felt piano, or did John Cage's prepared piano have something to do with it? How did Beuys's vision of Social Sculpture relate to the ideas of the rebellious counterculture of the late

Sixties? And what American artists interested him? Jackson Pol-
lock, because of his consideration of the energy problem, he told
me when I interviewed him in Oberkastel in 1983, and Warhol,
for his idea of the Factory.

Beuys' influence on American artists—on Robert Morris,
Richard Serra, Eva Hesse, and countless others—was also, for a
long time, a well-kept secret. "Morris was here. He worked in my
studio in 1963–64. He had an exhibition." In 1964 Beuys conceived a Fluxus performance in Berlin to be done simultaneously
in New York by Morris. Eva Hesse, who spent 1964–65 in Germany, also must have known Beuys's work; her own imagery of
human fragility at times parallels his. But Beuys must have been
influenced by American artists too. His piled squares of felt and
copper, the earliest dating from 1969, may reflect, formally at
least, the work of Carl Andre. And in June 1972, when Beuys lay
on the floor rubbing a piece of copper for several hours, in a
performance called "Vitus Agnus Castus," with the herb that's a
homeopathic remedy for excessive sexual desire fastened to his
hat, it may well have been a response to Vito Acconci's mastur-
batory "Seedbed" of January 1972.

As for Beuys' students—Jörg Immendorff, Imi Knoebel,
Anselm Kiefer, Walter Dahn—and the return to traditional can-
vas and paint: "Maybe they didn't really understand," Beuys
remarked to me in 1983. Besides the literal, the materialistic, the
cultural, and the messianic misunderstandings on both sides of
the ocean, there are historical ones. The circumstances of history
had put Beuys on the wrong side of a monstrous war. His art, to
many American viewers, seemed to expiate a guilty conscience.
Beuys said it wasn't so. "The enemy suffers too," he told me. His
work, he said, had nothing to do with guilt: it was rather an
exhortation to remember that everyone suffers. In America he

generated both adulation and hostility, as would-be saviors do. Yet he showed artists here in the Seventies and Eighties that an artist could be activist as well as theorist, and showman as well as shaman. Did he bring the message of a politicized art to America when he arrived in 1974 during the energy crisis? Or did his ideas simply coincide with and reinforce the anti-formal, anti-establishment, postconceptual concerns already here?

With Beuys, the modern myth of the artist—half-crazed visionary, half surrogate god—that began with Van Gogh and ended with Warhol, reached its peculiar peak. "All roads of art pass through the thickets of that nut's mind one way or the other," commented a fellow critic at an opening a few years ago. "He's so dour, with that maniacal sense of humor, but boy, he has certainly turned European art around," said another. Beuys may have been the last of the old-time German Expressionists or he may have been the first universal postmodern man, or both. His effect on the art of our waning century is incalculable. In his work the issue of survival coexists with the optimistic fiction of progress. As for his belief in the therapeutic powers of art, it gives new meaning to Matisse's remark about art as a comfy armchair.

Beuys in America, or
The Energy Plan for the Western Man

CAROLINE TISDALL

Beuys' initial impression of the United States was of its inno-
cence. During his first visit to New York at the age of fifty-three
he was constantly reminded of his childhood in the small German town of Kleve in the late Twenties. He had stepped back in
time. "New York is the most innocent town in the world. It looks
as if it were made of children's building blocks, and the shops
have a naive glamour I remember well from the Roaring
Twenties."[1]

It was typical of Beuys that for his first appearance in the
United States he should choose to present "The Energy Plan for
the Western Man," nothing less. Not an exhibition or a "lecture
tour," but an Energy Plan. This was January 1974, just two years
after he had been dismissed from his professorship in the Kunstakademie in Düsseldorf. He had been sacked for defying Nume-

---

[1]Caroline Tisdall, notebooks (unpublished), 1974

7

rus Clausus (restricted entry) in the German higher education system, and devoted much time and energy in the next few years to travelling and talking to as many people in as many places as possible. His basic principle was that those who feel they have something to teach and those who feel they have something to learn have the right to come together.

The "Energy Plan" was part of the thinking behind the Free International University for Creativity and Interdisciplinary Research, which Beuys and the Nobel Prize-winning novelist Heinrich Böll, among others, had founded in Düsseldorf after his dismissal in 1972. Their conviction was that creativity is the key to change and evolution *and* that it cannot be restricted to a narrow group of specialists called artists. "I'm not here to speak about the particular problems of artists, but about the whole question of potential, the possibility that everybody can do his own particular kind of art and work for the new social organization. Creativity is national income."[2]

That was part of his message to the restive audience at the New School in New York that January. For me too it was the first experience of the strangely expressionistic behavior of New York art world audiences. Beuys' old friend Willoughby Sharp was in the front row. He had been perhaps the first American to write about Beuys in his magazine "Avalanche." Now there he was yelling out "Vorsicht, Joseph!" as a warning whenever there was a hostile question.

Beuys had refused to go to the United States while the Vietnam War was on. Now that he was in New York it was inevitable that his wartime past as a Stuka pilot in the German Luftwaffe

---

[2]Joseph Beuys at The New School for Social Research, New York City, January 1974

would attract the attention of some of the audience. It was during such moments that the seeds for the dialogue with the coyote were sown in Beuys' mind! But this first encounter with the American audience had been billed as a "dialogue" too. Among the artists in the audience at the New School were those, like Al Hanson, who grew impatient: "I was invited to a dialogue, but you're sending us to sleep," and others who wanted to join in and make the whole thing into performance art.

There was some confusion of terms. For Beuys this was not "performance," but "social sculpture," a means of suggesting and effecting change beyond restricted art concepts. "I feel it is important to appear with nothing now in order to get closer to people, to make contact, to take a step away from alienation towards an organic alternative. ... The energy of the mental process gives the energy for a change in physical actions."[3] In Europe in the Seventies there was much more sense of the need for social change than this audience conceded. Beuys was talking about a sense of crisis perhaps not felt in New York: "The human body is a microcosm of the world. In times of crisis we feel our being to be threatened (sic). We must get beyond the body to achieve an outside view of the world."[4]

There was a strongly spiritual dimension to Beuys' "Energy Plan for the Western Man." He referred to historic figures like the Renaissance philosopher Campanella who envisaged the "Sun State:" "One day man like a god will create his own planet—a spiritual state."[5] Such things were said with full knowledge of the suspended disbelief they aroused in those listeners of a purely

[3]ibidem
[4]ibidem
[5]ibidem

materialist mind: At the same time Beuys always emphasized the perfectly plausible possibility that human beings are in a state of evolution, that there may be things to come of which we cannot dream, hence Beuys' "Warmth Ferry" and "Warm Time Machine," both expressions of the human capacity for warmth and love. "We have reached a stage of evolution where all these things will come together . . ."[6]

Beuys had great faith in the human capacity to find answers to problems. In Chicago a few days later, talking at the School of the Art Institute, he found an audience whose response to philosophical problems was certainly more engaged than in New York. Encouraged by their interest and much deeper level of questioning, he expanded the spiritual theme. Of all the lectures I heard him give in those years, in Europe or America, this was the one in which the relationship in Beuys' thinking between the spiritual, social and natural worlds was clearest. The blackboards he drew in Chicago were extraordinarily beautiful, so much so that we used details of the "Sun State" board photographs for the cover of the original "Secret Block for a Secret Person in Ireland" catalog later that year.

Threefold structure was a theme that fascinated Beuys. He had pursued triads, trinities and triangles through his studies of Western philosophy, early Christianity and natural science from the Holy Trinity through alchemy and on to Rudolf Steiner and the "From the people, by the people, for the people" of Abraham Lincoln's Gettysburg Address, which now seemed very apposite. He saw threefold form as governing natural structure and human nature, and it recurs throughout his sculpture, drawings and actions.

---

[6]ibidem

The theory of Social Sculpture by which Beuys described the process of creation was based on three stages: the passage from chaotic energy and unformed mass through a process of harmony and molding to a determined and crystallized form. It was a principle he applied in different contexts, as was his adaptation of Steiner's anthroposophic description of the three main areas of social organization.

When Beuys drew a plant or a human figure in the Energy Plan lectures he was describing the different capacities for thinking, feeling and will. According to Steiner, the organization of society into the three main areas of economics, law and culture best describes the use of these capacities. The human being, according to Beuys' diagram, carries his spiritual roots on his head and is "fed from above." A plant is the other way up, drawing its main "food" from the earth. The human sex organs are lower down the body (the old-fashioned "nether regions"), while in plants they are on top, and so on.

While looking round the Art Institute, we had come across a drawing by the great architectural designer Louis Sullivan. It was a page from Sullivan's "Theory of Ornament," a wonderful piece of draftsmanship illustrating the importance of natural design in ornamentation. Sullivan had entitled the drawing "The Aspect of Freedom is Beginning to Appear." For Beuys it was the kind of omen to which he was always very open on his travels. Sullivan had added: "Manipulation of variants on a given axial theme."

Beuys incorporated these messages from Sullivan into the Energy Plan. Freedom after all was the underlying theme of his work and self-determination was his political ideal. "All systems are oppressive because they are abstract and concerned only with how a minority can govern. . . . There can never be repression as long as you are a thinker . . . The original idea of Christianity 'I will make you free' had to do with changing the world, before it was institutionalized."[7]

Beuys was a ferocious opponent of ideology when it restricted the freedom of the individual. He believed passionately in the individual's right to develop his or her own capacities and creativity. He was equally firm in his criticism of eccentric behavior, particularly of the kind often displayed by artists—and which he had encountered in New York: "The ego must be developed, not for its own sake, but because it is needed by society. If you are only interested in self-realization then you cannot make a good painting. To do this you have to have thought about forming, and about how ideas of forming stem from history."[8]

Louis Sullivan was not the only gift Chicago made to Beuys. Driving round looking (in vain) for traces of his relatives from Kleve who had settled as bakers in Chicago in the early Thirties, we came across the Biograph cinema, and the John Dillinger legend. Another German of course, a gangster gunned down here: "The negative energies in him could have led to a positive impulse. Instead they became subhuman. Our impulse of love for such people is superhuman . . ."[9] The "Dillinger" video with its soundtrack of Beuys laughing was the result. Once again he was close to the time and aura of his childhood, and a step closer to the thinking behind "Coyote."

By January 16th we were in Minneapolis where Beuys spoke at the College of Art and Design. The most dominant impression he had of the college was of its amazing rubber floor in the huge

[7]Joseph Beuys at the School of the Art Institute of Chicago, January 1974
[8]ibidem
[9]Caroline Tisdall, notebooks as above

video studio, but he was not overwhelmed by such physical equipment: "This kind of art school is for me the least important. A spiritual structure is needed. If a person is an artist he can use the most primitive of instruments:—a broken knife is enough. Otherwise it remains a craft school."[10] He was thinking, of course, of his own efforts to establish the most basic of interdisciplinary schools.

The first journey was organized by Ronald Feldman. When Beuys returned to New York in May 1974 it was to show support for the opening of René Block's gallery in SoHo. Block had been a long-time enthusiast of the Fluxus movement, and his Berlin gallery had been the venue for the early Beuys action "The Chief" in 1964. Now Block was among the first of a new generation of Europeans to try his luck in New York, and Beuys arrived for the coyote action.

The subtitle was a neat piece of (self-)mockery: "I like America and America likes me." It had been clear on the first visit that there were quite a few people who did not like Beuys! Enough to remember Harold Rosenberg's comment on first encountering a Beuys drawing at the Ronald Feldman gallery: "One thing is for sure: this artist cannot draw." The America Beuys had loved on his winter journey had been the icy landscapes of Labrador, the north winds of the Chicago lakeshore, in contrast to the steam rising from sheets of iron and subway vents on the streets of New York, the America of Dillinger and the old billboard ads: "A square deal to all. . . . Money back within seven days," the world of "Shopping bag interests, pension interests and insurance swindles" as Beuys called it.

In choosing the coyote Beuys was seeking a dialogue with a different America, as he explains in the extract from my

---

[10]ibidem

"Coyote" book quoted on page 141. The coyote was a powerful deity for the North American Indian, a wily and highly versatile character as described in Jung's Pueblo Indian tales. Behind Beuys' choice was the hounding of the coyote/Indian by the white man who recast him as a mean criminal, a technique known as "Europe of the pogroms" as Beuys pointed out.

Along with "How to Explain Pictures to a Dead Hare," the coyote action has the greatest appeal to people, and has acquired even more relevance as environmental awareness and respect for other species increases. It had a magic of timing, light and rhythm about it that was sustained throughout each day of performance. The apparent effortlessness of the encounter and the relaxed atmosphere were in spite of all sorts of difficulties sown in the path of the dialogue by the New York Department of Health, attempts by the police at Kennedy to arrest the ambulance in which the felt-swathed Beuys was being driven to meet the coyote. ("Who gave you folks the authority to disrupt the traffic?" asked the irate cop after a siren chase. "Gee, I haven't enjoyed myself so much since Vietnam," replied the ambulance driver.) When we reached the gallery in SoHo Beuys decided the felt was of too poor a quality: "That's shoddy, not felt"; the floor of lovely old wood had been over-cleaned; and the fence separating man and wolf from the public was too petit-bourgeois: "A Mondrian fence!"[11] Two days passed before all was ready. Beuys was a perfectionist, and people understood the demands he made on them because he was just as demanding of himself. When it happened, "Coyote" was "perfect."

A year later, in April, 1975, he was back, to show *"Richtkräfte"* (Directional Forces) at the René Block Gallery and *"Feuerstelle"*

---

[11]ibidem

(Hearth) at Ronald Feldman Fine Arts, both major pieces of environmental sculpture "built" in Europe rather than owing anything specific to Beuys' experience of America. It was not until "News from the Coyote" shown during the huge Beuys show at the Solomon R. Guggenheim Museum which I curated in 1979, that anything specifically "American" was added to his work. "News from the Coyote" was a deeply melancholy environment, a gallery-wide barrier of asbestos-infested rubble from the now defunct René Block Gallery, softly lamp-lit and with the "Coyote" instruments, gloves, triangle, felt and Wall Street Journals, laid to rest. By then Beuys was as well-known as he was ever likely to be in America.

SOCIAL SCULPTURE

I

"Introduction"
1979

My objects are to be seen as stimulants for the transformation of the idea of sculpture . . . or of art in general. They should provoke thoughts about what sculpture can be and how the concept of sculpting can be extended to the invisible materials used by everyone.

THINKING FORMS—	how we mold our thoughts or
SPOKEN FORMS—	how we shape our thoughts into words or
SOCIAL SCULPTURE—	how we mold and shape the world in which we live: SCULPTURE AS AN EVOLUTIONARY PROCESS; EVERYONE AN ARTIST.

That is why the nature of my sculpture is not fixed and finished. Processes continue in most of them: chemical reactions, fermentations, color changes, decay, drying up. Everything is in a STATE OF CHANGE.

19

"I am searching for field character"
1973

Only on condition of a radical widening of definition will it be possible for art and activities related to art to provide evidence that art is now the only evolutionary-revolutionary power. Only art is capable of dismantling the repressive effects of a senile social system that continues to totter along the deathline: to dismantle in order to build A SOCIAL ORGANISM AS A WORK OF ART.

This most modern art discipline—Social Sculpture/Social Architecture—will only reach fruition when every living person becomes a creator, a sculptor, or architect of the social organism. Only then would the insistence on participation of the action art of FLUXUS and Happening be fulfilled; only then would democracy be fully realized. Only a conception of art revolutionized to this degree can turn into a politically productive force, coursing through each person, and shaping history.

But all this, and much that is as yet unexplored, has first to form part of our consciousness: insight is needed into objective

21

connections. We must probe (theory of knowledge) the moment of origin of free individual productive potency (creativity). We then reach the threshold where the human being experiences himself primarily as a spiritual being, where his supreme achievements (work of art), his active thinking, his active feeling, his active will, and their higher forms, can be apprehended as sculptural generative means, corresponding to the exploded concepts of sculpture divided into its elements—indefinite—movement—definite (see theory of sculpture), and are then recognized as flowing in the direction that is shaping the content of the world right through into the future.

This is the concept of art that carries within itself not only the revolutionizing of the historic bourgeois concept of knowledge (materialism, positivism), but also of religious activity.

EVERY HUMAN BEING IS AN ARTIST who—from his state of freedom—the position of freedom that he experiences at first-hand—learns to determine the other positions in the TOTAL ARTWORK OF THE FUTURE SOCIAL ORDER. Self-determination and participation in the cultural sphere (freedom); in the structuring of laws (democracy); and in the sphere of economics (socialism). Self-administration and decentralization (threefold structure) occurs: FREE DEMOCRATIC SOCIALISM.

THE FIFTH INTERNATIONAL is born

Communication occurs in reciprocity: it must never be a one-way flow from the teacher to the taught. The teacher takes equally from the taught. So oscillates—at all times and everywhere, in any conceivable internal and external circumstance, between all degrees of ability, in the work place, institutions, the street, work circles, research groups, schools—the master/pupil, transmitter/receiver, relationship. The ways of achieving this are manifold, corresponding to the varying gifts of individuals and groups. THE ORGANIZATION FOR DIRECT DEMOCRACY THROUGH REFERENDUM is one such group. It seeks to launch many similar work groups or information centers, and strives towards world-wide cooperation.

A public dialogue
New York City
1974

Beuys made his first visit to the United States from January 9 through January 19, 1974 at the invitation of Ronald Feldman Fine Arts Inc. and Dayton's Gallery 12. He spent five days in New York and on January 11th at 8 P.M. conducted a Public Dialogue at the New School to a packed auditorium of 350 people. Several hundred more people were crowded outside the doors and trying to get in. The following is a near-verbatim transcript of the first hour of the dialogue, which lasted for nearly three hours.

JOSEPH BEUYS: I would be very glad if there were a possibility, later, to speak to the public outside . . .

I was invited to come here to speak about my idea of art, which is to enlarge the effectivity of art beyond the idea of art as coming out of art history—an art idea which contains the well-known disciplines like sculpture, architecture, painting, music, dancing, poetry and so on. I would like to declare why I feel that it's now necessary to establish a new kind of art, able to show the problems of the whole society, of every living being—and how this new discipline—which I call social sculpture—can realize the future of humankind. It could be a guarantee for the evolution of the earth as a planet, establish conditions for other planetarians too, and you can control it with your own thinking . . . But first, before we begin with the discussion and the dialogue—and it would be very nice if the dialogue could be very intensive—let me show in general the structure of this thinking.

In trying to change from one well-known ideology to another, you have to develop a methodology by looking at phenomena in reality. And all these have to be related step by step to the social structure. We have first to ask, in what part of the social structure does art live? Art as an element in the whole culture is normally placed at the point of creativity. But we have to see what creativity means for the whole. Perhaps this is easier to do if we consider the element of freedom in creativity—let me go a bit quicker through the ideas, it doesn't matter if at first it's a little unsharp. At present this area has a special place in the society, and there are other areas in which to work, the law structure, economics . . .

Here my idea is to declare that art is the *only* possibility for evolution, the only possibility to change the situation in the world. But then you have to enlarge the idea of art to include the whole creativity. And if you do that, it follows logically that every living being is an artist—an artist in the sense that he can develop his own capacity. And therefore it's necessary at first that society cares about the educational system, that equality of opportunity for self-realization is guaranteed.

Under the present educational structure in the Western world, in private capitalistic systems, this is not guaranteed. So research into a new political structure has to go on at the same time. But the term politics, in the light of what I have just said, has another content. It means now a kind of art. And therefore, in short, I'm saying, all work that's done has to have the quality of art. We can see later about developing a proof for this by thinking about these problems. Here is a general structure to show what I mean by a social sculpture.

(Beuys goes to blackboard and points out symbols for archetypal elements, plants, animals, minerals, soul which he had drawn before the discussion started.)

There is now already a question in the audience, and perhaps it would be good to begin with this question.

First questioner: Have you ever thought of using holography as a medium? *(Audience giggles.)*

BEUYS: I have heard of this word "holography," but I am not very well acquainted with this kind of science. But perhaps it isn't a science.

Q: It is a kind of science, but there are artists like Dali, Robert Indiana, who have used it as an art medium.

BEUYS: This science could have similar interests to my interests, to look for the whole, if you say *holo* from the Greek *holos*, meaning the whole. But I'm not very well-informed about it. Could you maybe give an example of how holography thinks about the idea of art as a means for shaping the future? Is holography only a special science, or can holography supply models for the social structure? For questions in economics, or how to work with money. *(Audience laughter.)*

No, I ask only these questions because we have to slowly, step by step—and when I say slowly, I mean as soon as possible, yes— (*loud laughter*) but it has to be done carefully, one step after the other, only then can we catch a bit from the whole very complex thing. I dared to begin with, and to introduce the whole problematic from this field ... to say that art is the only evolutionary power for history, that art is the only field that could govern the whole of society. Not only this, that it is not right, as nowadays practiced, that politicians and managers of economic powers control the destinies of the majority. We can later return to these terms and make proofs in thinking to see if I am right in saying this. Now you are perhaps clear (*general laughter, good humored*) or better able to speak about the idea of holography. When I hear this word, I feel a good thing, ya! (*Laughter and applause. To another member of audience:*) You are invited too!

SECOND QUESTIONER: I think first of all there is enormous outside pressure going on, I do not understand why people cannot sit here in the aisles. (*Clapping*).

BEUYS: There is the fire police, you know.

RONALD FELDMAN: If we wish to continue to use the auditorium tonight, we have to respect fire regulations ...

Q: In the back there is a constant noise going on of people.

RONALD FELDMAN: I'm sorry, you'll have to bear with us.

Q: (*from the floor*) If Mister Beuys is a social artist, as he says he is, (*audience boos loudly, cries of let him talk, let him talk, general commotion*) I don't want to come on stage because I feel that er ... I don't see evidence that this type of social gathering is effective for the communication of an artist's ideas, which could be done perhaps better through the use of media. *Let me finish, let me finish. (Let him speak.)* . . . The people who organized this . . . *(Be quiet, let him speak.)*

BEUYS: But I think you have to ask if your action now is productive for the whole, yes, that's the kind of holography . . . *(general laughter, applause, right on, that got rid of him).*

But perhaps you are right with your attitude. First we have to ask whether there is a possibility that this discussion could take place, and perhaps you can analyze later whether I am a social artist or not. You know, that could be the result of the free discussion. But first you have to ask yourself whether your intervention is productive for the whole. What you did just now was a kind of critique, yes. And I'm saying, is critique the only method to find a solution for the questions we all have in the society? *(Aaaah . . . applause).* If you only criticize . . . But you are invited to come here [to the stage] and speak about the problems.

Q: Here's one solution: is it possible to amplify the discussion that's going on here so that it can be heard outside without the people moving in?

THIRD QUESTIONER: *(shouts from his seat)* You said . . . that art is the most important motive force in history. *(No no no).* That's a subjectivist point of view. It differs for example from Darwin . . . *(laughter).*

BEUYS: No, I did not say this.

Q: If art is the most important force in history, then Tolstoy becomes a very important person because there is no access from the left for a subjective point of view in relation to art, except Tolstoy. *(Loud guffaws)* Tolstoy was used as an authority in

Russia, and he collaborated with Bertrand Russell (*screams of laughter, Caroline Tisdall, writer for* The Guardian, *translates into German . . . whistling and clapping*) Mrs. Browning was plagiarized by Oscar Wilde (*Caroline explains gist of this rap to Beuys in German. Reference to Mrs. Browning provokes more laughter and applause . . . What do you mean?*) The question of time is in abeyance. In Russia they have time, due to the five-year plan. (*Whistling and clapping*). The motion is that the fine arts lead the mechanical arts . . .

FOURTH QUESTIONER: (*picks up mike*) Does this work? I would like to address Mr. Beuys with the following question. In many respects I think he may have many valuable things to say as an artist (*Whew! Audience laughs at questioner.*) I know his work briefly (*more incredulous laughter*) but I don't think that's a criterion for thinking he has much to offer. Judging from the number of people who have gathered here as well as outside, the idea of a social force—in view of the physical pressure on this structure architecturally—I'm talking about a social phenomenon—I think it's very difficult to maintain a dialogue, social, artistic or otherwise, without some regard for the fact that people are waiting . . . and there's a social danger of people fighting and actually trying to break in and getting hurt in the process. I think that's of prime concern as an artist. What I suggest is that the media should get their artistic capabilities together and present this in a manner (*Audience shouts: It's being taped!*) . . . Taping is a possibility. There are many media possibilities for presenting Mr. Beuys' ideas to the public. (*Don't waste time now! Thank you, thank you!*) I would like to ask Mr. Beuys whether he has a social concern for the people outside. Would you consider holding this at a future time? (*He said he would, he said he would, let*

him speak!) I'll leave as soon as I have my word ... (*Finish!
Finish! Off the stage! Clapping, cheers.*)

BEUYS: Yes, you see how dangerous a discussion can be ...
(*cheers*) It would be better for the whole discussion if you could
come to the stage, otherwise everyone begins to talk.

Q: (*angry*) I'm going to leave now because I don't believe a
meaningful dialogue can take place here. (*Audience applauds
approvingly. Commotion*).

FIFTH QUESTIONER: I came here to listen to the philosophy of
Mr. Beuys. He speaks elusively, and what I'd like is clarification
of a lot of the points he's made on the blackboard. (*Clapping*). I'd
like to lead him through a question or two, as long as you want to
tolerate it. The first one is, why did he put art higher than
religion and science?

BEUYS: I work in the field of art, and you know how during a
period of Marxist ideology, fewer people are inclined to believe in
the power of the culture as a whole: they believe in the revolutionary potential of economics, class struggle theory ... Therefore it's time to show that art means the power of creativity, and
it's time to define art in a larger way, to include science and
religion too. I mentioned that already at the beginning, but I
know how difficult it is to understand too many ideas ... You
have only to look at the phenomena, and to think without
prejudice, to see the mostly simply and monumental errors that
nowadays characterize politics. That's the beginning of the process ...

SIXTH QUESTIONER: Is your art socialistic? In what sense is your
art tied to socialism?

BEUYS: But what is socialistic art? That is not what I mean.

Q: Oh. Then why is art connected to socialism? I don't understand. Do you mean the artist can exist only in a socialist society? *(No, no, audience cries.)*

BEUYS: No. I mean the idea of art has to be changed. And you have to look for the springpoint, where the creative principle begins. Art as it's now understood is a special kind of creativity; there are others, like philosophy or electricity. But it's very simple to see that all these activities are necessary for (designating) things in the world. An electrician, a physicist or a doctor has to form the problems he finds in the world, yes? But if you want to provide a fundamental analysis of these problems, you have to develop a special kind of consciousness-science. And then you find that the human being isn't only located in a physical context, that he isn't only incarnated in the physical world between birth and death . . . his thinking springs from another source. So we should not understand art as coming from complicated material processes; you find the person outside of conditions in the physical environment. The whole problematic of understanding the function of art in the society is to change our understanding of ourselves and humankind—the problem is only to understand that man is first a being who needs nourishment for his spiritual needs, and that if he could cultivate and train this primary nature, this spiritual nature, he could develop whole other energies. In this way the whole plan is a kind of energy plan too.

And I'm saying that artists working in the West and East and Far East, cannot arrive at a good result unless they look first to the point from where creativity springs. And you see culture related to freedom, because culture implies freedom: there can be no repression from any point. If there is a situation like now in Soviet Russia, where a writer like Solzhenitsyn is repressed by the system, because he expressed a special result from his research—I'm using the term in an interdisciplinary way, because I want to give art the effectivity of the whole creativity. Then I can give it more power and force, I can catch all the participants who are already researching, widen the direction for all people—I mean the majority in an equal way. And when I say freedom, I mean freedom for thinking and researching and expressing the meaning (of that research and thought). And no political power has the right to oppress any individual . . . But perhaps . . .

SEVENTH QUESTIONER: You talk a little bit like Nietzsche, but you're favorable to socialism, whereas he hated it. Your idea of art freeing people . . .

BEUYS: I hate socialism too when it's only mentioned in a vacuum. The results of socialism you can see in special places. What does it mean? Socialism means nothing, unless all the powers you find in human nature for freedom, equality, and brotherhood are included in the context of socialism. Socialism, democracy, freedom alone mean nothing, because freedom tends to become chaos when there are not orders established through a democratic decision by all people together, when there is not a border to chaotic activity, when everyone could do what he wants—dying too, murdering, all these things . . .

There has to be a structure of laws, but not established from above by a minority of politicians or by economic interests. The basic law structure or the constitution has to be realized by the majority—it means an elementary democratic process. And that's only possible when everyone participates. But for this it needs a special ability: you have to learn how the democratic process functions. And this is where you have to look to the culture, and ask whether we now have a cultural structure which allows everyone to learn equally and freely to be conscious of and make new decisions (relating to) all the problems.

EIGHTH QUESTIONER: Getting away from politics, are you developing a new aesthetic for your own art?

BEUYS: This is *my* understanding of aesthetics: I don't say that everyone has to believe my thinking. I am not the only researcher in this field, there are more and more people who want to research in this direction: I only want to provide an impulse for this kind of thinking, I don't want it to be construed as a dogma. That would be directly opposed to what I want.

Q: How would you describe your new aesthetic?

BEUYS: I describe it *radically*: I say aesthetics = human being. That is a radical formula. I set the idea of aesthetics directly in the context of human existence, and then I have the whole problem in the hand, then I have not a special problem, I have a "holography." (*Beuys laughs, audience laughs, sympathetically.*) I don't know exactly what holography is . . . (*more laughter*).

Q: You mentioned a form of classless society where this form of education would be possible. Now do you consider art as a result or a procedure to attain this classless society?

BEUYS: I think art is the only political power, the only revolutionary power, the only evolutionary power, the only power to free humankind from all repression. I say not that art has already realized this, on the contrary, and because it has not, it has to be developed as a weapon—at first there are radical levels, then you can speak about special details.

Q: But I feel it's a kind of vicious circle: then you want to use art as the aim and the strategy (*Loud banging on the doors*). But the people here in New York, we are just a bourgeois elite (*laughter*) so—I'm not attacking you—why not talk with the workers or the Blacks in Harlem?

BEUYS: Why not? To this situation they are invited in an equal way. We have to go step by step. But why have they no interest to come? Because they are not accustomed to look for [this kind of] invitation in the newspaper, or to look for the posters. They have not learned to. The majority perhaps is in this position, they don't know the value of culture. Their alienation means that they are not aware of their own needs for mental nourishment. For instance, in a special ideology the needs of the majority are expressed by the idea of alienation. But exactly this alienation is where culture doesn't have a place—in factories, in the whole economic structure . . .

For this reason I try to develop social sculpture as a new discipline in art—at first it is an invisible sculpture, and it's very uncommon to look for invisible sculpture. You see, I come to the United States as a sculptor, and the sculpture is to see nothing in the gallery of Ronald Feldman. I want to take sculpture in this direction: alienation has to be exchanged for a warm element . . .

Q: You speak about alienation of workers in the factories, but don't you feel that coming to New York City at the invitation of a gallery alienates you to the same extent, because it makes you a prisoner of the art world? Because you are both in the same boat, if you want to free yourselves.

BEUYS: I don't understand. (*Caroline Tisdall translates into German*: Kunstwelt.)

BEUYS: You mentioned a good term. You can go, as an artist, into the ivory tower situation . . .

Q: That's not what I mean. People have come here to listen to you, not because they believe you are going to start another revolution, but because you are a curiosity as an artist, and they came here more for aesthetic reasons than political, or at least half the people who came here that I know.

BEUYS: You have only to ask yourself why you came here! (*Audience shouts, right, right!*)

Q: I asked a friend of mine why she came, and she said, because she liked your picture on the poster. (*Audience laughs.*)

BEUYS: (*grins*) And why not! (*Applause*).

NINTH QUESTIONER: I'm having a hard time dealing with what you have to say about art, because you've managed to make it so all-encompassing, so holistic (*audience groans at obvious pun*) that you haven't been able to define its boundaries. What *are* the boundaries?

BEUYS: At first I am more interested in destroying the narrow boundaries that come from a historical understanding of art. All these things in the past were not able to fulfill what Picasso demanded, that art has to be a weapon for all people . . .

Q: But you still haven't defined any parameters, any edges. What I think you're saying is that a discipline has to have a problem in order for someone to operate. A doctor can't fix someone unless he's sick.

BEUYS: No, that for me is a very poor thing (*laughter*). Then you run the danger of constructing a problem. But I am a phenomenologist—I look for the reality of the phenomenon. You have only to look—you have eyes, you have a sensory organization. This is another point of research: what is the sense construction in human beings, how is the nervous system organized, what is its capacity for reception? There is no need to construct problems, they are there outside . . .

Q: You said that art should encompass all the other disciplines, should become interdisciplinary. Aren't you making art the new politics?

BEUYS: Yes, surely. Politics has to become art, and art has to become politics. That's exactly the point I'm making: all human activities have to become art, and they have to be organized by artists . . .
(Second tape, side one: first part is inaudible.)

TENTH QUESTIONER: I wanted to know why you haven't been to the United States prior to this visit now. Was there some requirement that the country had to meet, in its attitude or its morals, before you would visit it?

BEUYS: *(Caroline Tisdall calls out, Joseph, Joseph, microphone! It's hard to hear.)* I had the opportunity to come earlier, but the invitations always specified that I had to do something special, make a work for exhibition, they were connected to the wishes of a special person. And during this period, I no longer had an interest in exhibiting. And so I didn't come, not because I have anything against the United States, but I had too much to do in Germany . . . Then Ronald Feldman invited me, to do nothing in the gallery, invisible sculpture . . .

"I put me on this train!"
interview with Art Papier
1979

ART PAPIER: Joseph Beuys, do you have a mission?

JOSEPH BEUYS: Yes, perhaps I have a mission . . . to change the social order. To change the money system mostly, that's the most important thing, the money system. Money and the state are the only oppressive powers in the present time. Money and the state and the [interaction] between these blocks. There *is* no other power and as long as people go to vote and go to the polling booths and say yes, yes, yes, to this system, as long this system will survive. And so we go radically another way and push against this. *Radically.*

PAPIER: I heard you say in a recent television interview that you don't look towards America for this kind of radical social transformation, that you feel that Germany or Central Europe will probably be the place where it can happen, because in Germany change can happen more quickly.

39

BEUYS: This is what I think. It is only an estimation, you see, I was not judging. I said probably. Now this the sixth time I've been in the United States, with dialogues, with actions, now with a kind of exposition. I have in the meantime had some experience with the American scene and I admire and I like America. Like on the poster that was to be seen: "I like America and America likes me." That's true, but I feel that in Central Europe, at the moment there is much more tension and much more power in the discussion about the future of society. So I feel Europe will maybe, perhaps or probably, be the spot where the new ideas come up, in the next one, two, three years; that's what I think.

PAPIER: And this process will come through a democratic change, will involve direct democracy?

BEUYS: Yes sure, that is what I think. I am against the kind of revolution done from one day to the other, with a kind of *putsch* character, you know. So I'm working in a more revolutionary way, going the organic way, finding as much as possible people supporting such a movement, so I try with a movement on the grass roots . . . against the ruling systems not only in Central Europe but in every part of the continent. . . . A democratic system is already working, with more . . . and more minorities working on their grass-roots problems, pushing against the system. I see already running within the Free International University or in similarly shaped organizations, the impact and the results of a kind of direct democracy.

PAPIER: None of what I've seen or read [about your work] speaks directly to the political realities of your life. Yesterday, I heard you talk about the evils of economic profit in philosophical terms. Let's talk about profit in terms of your show at the Guggenheim Museum. What does this exhibition mean politically and economically for you?

BEUYS: Politically, it means perhaps a lot because there is a good impact in West Germany. If a person like me does succeed in a foreign country, and especially in New York, in the United States, and at the Guggenheim, it brings a lot of impact to people who are in a way enemies of my intentions in the cultural scene, in democratic discussions, in economic proposals.

PAPIER: Economically, in the long run, this can mean a lot for your work?

BEUYS: It could mean a lot for my work on the side of business and on the whole side of the economic value of objects. But because, and since, I am no longer working in the object, in making *things*, and I am working more promoting political ideas within West Germany and other countries, like the Netherlands, England, and Italy, I will surely not be a producer of objects which [make] money on the art market. But, on the other hand, I have to care for money because the whole organization of the Free International University, for instance, needs money. Every person who is involved with the Free International University doesn't take an income from the organization. Everybody involved has another profession from where he takes his income. So we try to establish a kind of internal bank system where everybody gives as much as possible to the pool.

PAPIER: So you give a lot of your money to the Free International University, to this pool?

BEUYS: Yes, sure.

PAPIER: Does this increase your power with the Free International University?

BEUYS: The Free International University is a political movement. And during election processes like the election of the European parliaments and now, with the coming federal election in West Germany, we surely are in very bad condition if we have to raise money. For instance, information in the streets, actions, going on trips with the material, speaking in different towns and all such activities, cost a lot of money. Therefore, we need a kind of pooling system. And I try to do as much as I can to fill in because I sometimes have a better income than other people. Sometimes, it's a big quantity I can give, sometimes it's less, you know. This relates to the production of art articles—giving in the art market—so I cannot completely stop this production of sculptures, art objects, which result in this capitalistic system for money. One must see that I try to overcome the political system and try to develop a kind of enterprise, with other descriptions than the capitalistic enterprise and understood as a so-called free market, in business and all the other things. [For] surely every work has to be organized in a kind of enterprise or structure.

PAPIER: But doesn't that increase your importance in the Free International University, giving that money?

BEUYS: No, no, nobody has special importance in the Free International University. It is not a hierarchical organization.

PAPIER: You say in your manifesto for the Free International University that the traditional student/teacher relationship must be broken down, that it cannot be one-way, it has to be a dialogue, not a monologue.

BEUYS: That's exactly right.

PAPIER: Yet you remain at the center of the German Free International University. How important are you to the Free International University?

BEUYS: How important? I founded the Free International University. I shaped the idea. After I had done the Organization of Direct Democracy then later on I found it necessary to go on with a research enterprise and with a political movement related to every field of the society. Not only towards the ecological problems in democracy, but also to the freedom problem in creativity and then later in economics also, to change the understanding of money, to change the whole understanding of capital. Therefore, I founded the Free International University, but even though I founded the Free International University, I have no privilege in this organization. Everybody has a completely equal right, equal say, and there is no privilege. Everybody helps everybody as much as he can.

PAPIER: What I don't understand is: the Free International University is a democracy, you tell me everyone is important there, everyone has an equal say: then why so much attention on Joseph Beuys?

BEUYS: Yes, perhaps because I founded the whole idea and a lot of people feel it as a very radical intention to go and run this way. In a way it is a kind of innovation in the whole political discussion and also in the understanding of what art should or could do in the world as political power, art as a political power. Therefore, you see, it is in a way the *new* character of the things which makes people interested. And, on the other hand, it is surely the established information structure which tries to go the old way, which tries to work with the star . . .

PAPIER: But aren't you the star?

BEUYS: Yes, I am the star in a way. It's true. I admit this, but I try to use this position.

PAPIER: Do you encourage stardom?

BEUYS: No. Encourage it? I encourage the ability and the dignity, and the necessity to look at everybody's creativity.

PAPIER: You say you don't encourage stardom, but I see you publicly signing catalogs and posters. Your multiples cost a lot of money. People buy ownership of Joseph Beuys objects. The concepts seem very unimportant to these people.

BEUYS: But, you see, I don't judge about how people work, watching what they take out of catalogs, political manifestoes or things, I don't judge.

PAPIER: Okay, let's look at the multiples that are for sale in the museum. A $50 felt eraser with your signature—what intellectual, political value does that have?

BEUYS: It is a kind of vehicle, you know. It is a kind of making, spreading out ideas, that is what I think. It spreads out the idea. You must care for information and I personally try to make information available not only in a written way, in a logical description of the steps we should take in the future towards a liberal, equal and social society. I try also to work with images, with fantasy, with jokes, with humor. It accelerates the discussion of the problem of a new society. A new society is really something other than what some so-called socialists think the class struggle theory of Marx means. I think in a real other way of the future of society. You know, that is a problem. So I work coming from the idea of art as the most important means to transform the society.

PAPIER: You see yourself as being important in discussing these issues in the coming years. Do you think it is important for you to live a lifestyle that is consistent with your philosophical beliefs?

BEUYS: My lifestyle should be parallel to what I say, yes. I inform about possibilities, philosophies and ideas for life and future, and I cannot live radically another way, that would not be a very good example. But I think more and more people feel that I try at least, I try to do what should be in a way a kind of ideal. I can only say in this modest way I try to give what I can give. Yes, I try everyday new things. I try to be up and think over again what would be the next step and how I should behave. And so there is a moral intention also. It's implied in the whole thing. The morality of this thing is very important.

PAPIER: And you feel that your actions are consistent with your beliefs?

BEUYS: Yes, my actions are consistent during the last twenty-five years. But in every year I can see a kind of progress in details, I can see that there are a lot of details ameliorated in considering the problems for everyone's freedom in the cultural scene, also in education, schools, universities, information level, radio, television, newspapers. I see a progress in considering and research in the law, human rights question as a democratic power sphere, and during the last five to six years, the Free International

University. And with the help of very able friends and philosophers in Germany, [we can] develop the kind of economical model which would content the majority in that moment where the majority of the people can understand that this is a concrete and very solid proposal for a solution of the social question all over the world.

PAPIER: In your work for social transformation, do you want to avoid the profit system or be part of it?

BEUYS: No, I try to avoid the profit system . . . I am against the profit. But as long as I live in the capitalistic system I would be stupid to relinquish my money because I have to deal with the struggle against the system, and therefore I need the money to struggle against the profit system. But when the whole system is delivered by the majority of the people, and new laws are existing on the economical level avoiding every money thing, then everything is through. But as long as things are not through, I have to care for money to work against the system.

PAPIER: In that process, you come and have a show at the Guggenheim Museum in New York. They are also profiting from your show. For them politically it means a lot to have Joseph Beuys, the radical artist from West Germany come and show, for them it increases the image of the museum, in economic and political terms. Do you agree with that?

BEUYS: Sure, I think.

PAPIER: So at the same time you are feeding them.

BEUYS: No. Yes, I am feeding them, but feeding them also with new ideas. If you read the catalog then you see that the feeding process is also against the established position of this institution.

And because the whole world [consists] only of institutions one has no other thing to do than to go in with new ideas in the institution. Every family is already a kind of institution, yes, every person in itself is an institution. One can only work with institutions and bring other ideas [into] this institutional structure.

PAPIER: You say your ideas are new, if not radical and revolutionary, yet you get incredible support from the West German government. Why are they supporting you? If they are somewhat to the right, if not reactionary, why do they support you, a leftist artist, an artist who offers and suggests a whole new direction for society?

BEUYS: I don't know, perhaps they have the idea that it is necessary. That there is another reason to pay for the thing . . . No, they are not open-minded, but they have the fear of losing their face. Their system tries always to work with the image of their own particular freedom, pseudo-freedom. Everything is untrue, but they try to misuse the artists to make propaganda for what they call "we are free." So they also use the artist to make propaganda for their own system.

PAPIER: So they are using you?

BEUYS: Sure, they try to use me, but it is impossible to misuse me, because I go radically another way. I take their money out of their pools, and that's very interesting to do—and they should pay, the government should pay everything of the Free International University and then the thing would run. Very, very quickly and very easily you would reach another level of society.

PAPIER: So you will be the one to pull the money out and they don't really understand that you are going to put this money to a radical use.

BEUYS: At the moment they don't perhaps . . . In the meantime some people know already the system of which I work, I try to pull the money out of the system. But there are also examples of people who have more than other people—in a way privileged personalities—who try to change the system. There is not only the so-called underprivileged people interested in changing, but also people who have more money, rich people, are inclined to support such a movement. There is also a kind of what one calls in Germany *Maecenas*, who give a bit . . . sometimes more.

PAPIER: So there are people on the right who sympathize?

BEUYS: So what do you call right? Right and left doesn't exist, that's an illusion. Right and left doesn't exist anymore.

PAPIER: There are very wealthy people in Germany who support you?

BEUYS: They support the revolution.

PAPIER: They support the revolution. Doesn't that give them privileges? Now let me ask you this: is that a democracy, for them to use their money to influence the system? It means they have more power.

BEUYS: You say generally that all people that have more money are inclined to be against revolution. That's not true. Surely, the people who have more money are a minority, yes . . . [but] it is not the guilt of these single persons that they have more money, it is the guilt of everybody that they gain so much money. Therefore, if anyone is to be charged with guilt, one has only to look to themselves, to ourselves. Everybody is guilty in the system because everybody every morning has to ask: "How much do I work against the system? What did I organize against the system?" So everybody is guilty for the system and not [only] the so-called capitalist people who have more money than other people . . . If the people are clear that this use of capital in the society is a false one, why don't they rise from the grass roots and lay down their work? In the workers' factories, in Ford, Chrysler, in Germany in Mercedes-Benz, in the iron factory, in big business? No, as long as workers are supporting the capitalistic system, as long the capitalists will be there. And people with privilege and more money in their pockets—that's the system.

PAPIER: What role will you play in future politics?

BEUYS: In future politics I will play the role of a person who can show how money, capital, the idea of capital could change, away from an understanding of capital as a changing fate, where everybody's dignity is exchanged as a commodity, the so-called salary dependency. [To show] that money should shift to a democratic regulator of everybody's work, creativity and dignity. So I would call this kind of understanding of money, the dignity money, the ability money of the people. Therefore, the only need for democracy is to look for this and to see that [the] only means to change democracy is to change the understanding of money and the state. . . .

I can only work as an informer. I can only appear in different places, in universities, in the streets, during democratic processes, in election processes and speak about what I think about possibilities: how the future should be, should look, and how freedom should be organized. Equality in the democratic legal structure should be built up and the understanding of capital in economics should be radically changed. So I can only make information in a kind of program where people can see there is already a solution proposed. There are already existing morals.

PAPIER: That is your role, only as a teacher?

BEUYS: As a teacher, as an informer and an organizer who faces the people, who wishes, who could be perhaps, some influence in the parliament. That's my role now, to inform the people about possibilities, to organize the resistance against the system, and to organize elections. So I could run for a position in the parliament. I could, I did it already.

PAPIER: Are you interested in doing that in the future?

BEUYS: I am perhaps running for a federal election. I'm not really clear if this will then be the right decision, but I think it could run this way. Once sitting in the parliament, you have a lot of influence on the media; the media is then no longer able to push new ideas aside.

PAPIER: You seem to have a lot of influence on the media right now.

BEUYS: Yes, but you see every important political dimension of the thing gets cut out. They include only the traditional understanding of art and art activities in the given cultural scene, in the very boring, the "*nicht* existent" outside of the world and very far divided from the needs of the majority of the people. So I try to cut it out, and I try to bring it in—that's the only thing.

PAPIER: But why were you on the cover of a newsweekly, like *Der Spiegel?*

BEUYS: When I was five years old I was not on the cover, when I was thirty years old I was not on the cover, when I came out of the last World War I was not on the cover, when I made my first exposition I was, I think, thirty-four years old, I was not on the cover—even ten years later I was not on the cover—but with the propagation of a new understanding of art creativity and new understanding of art [working] towards social change, then I appeared slowly on the cover. I pushed it, I worked for this, I struggled for this, I put me on this train! Working in the streets, working in the open. So I made something from which the people felt, "Oh, let's look, there is an idea, perhaps very interesting to hear about" and so it came to the surface. I appeal only to the people to do similar things.

So at least, let me say I try, I try to do things as well as I can. And I can only encourage other people to do the same thing or similar things. This perhaps is a real other methodology because the whole movement can't be a conformity in itself. It has to be in a very manifold way, because what the system fears is manifoldness of people's intentions and inventions against the system. If you work with an ideology, for instance, a Marxist ideology, you will never succeed against the system. They take it over to their own things, yes, every system in the capitalistic system is already working inside with a kind of capitalistic sort. So the only methodology is the color, the manifoldness in the unity. The unity means the liberation of the people from the dependency of money and state in a given structure. So that's what I think.

Speech upon receiving an honorary doctorate degree from the Nova Scotia College of Art and Design, Halifax
1976

Dear friends, dear president, dear members of the staff, dear students, and dear parents of the students and dear all other people who are here now present with their self-conscious "I." I endeavor not to throw the dollop of fat on the table, the dollop, the complexity of the whole differentiated theory as is existent and developed in my work during the last ten years almost, as the theory of sculpture, as the "Energy Plan of the Western Man," as the "Warmth Ferry," as the "Sun State" and as the totalization of the idea of art. I stress the point after my greeting words to all of you who are present with your self-conscious "I" because already now I am standing on the basis of the problem of how an enlarged understanding of art could work and could break through the borders of isolation which the present culture stands in, isolated from or against all other fields of society, such as the whole democratic energy field, the economic energy field.

Here I am standing now in the language problem and in the basic problem of the inspired speaker, since I stress being present with the self-conscious "I." As a starting point when I come to the desk here I invent my beginning as only a normal living being, as only a natural person. But already in being interested to speak to you, to the audience, to the people, to the receiver, since I can speak with sense; then I speak already not only as a natural person but I also speak as an engaged person. In this manner I am not only describing as a natural person can describe but I am also describing and determining a "me." I speak already as an interested ego, and I am more interested in the receiver.

I'm here standing in the field of relations and communications. In this field already appears the whole ability of the people working together in communication, bringing together all different abilities in experiences of life with results of research, with results of investigation. This field contains already an indefinite number of different problems. It is, it appears as, a kind of addition, an endless addition of all problems contained already in the problem of cultural doings. But to go on with this being interested, to go on to stress the element of relationship and communication as a democratic love process in language, I must bore or drill deeper to the thought level of the self-conscious "I" because only this position in consciousness can find a united substance with the ability to metamorphize the conditions in the society, which are no other things than a collection of sometimes already dead things or old things and which therefore work like an illness in society and work like a cancer, especially in the process of creating freedom. I cannot understand the idea of creativity where it is not related to the self-conscious "I" which stands in the field of inner freedom.

From this basic position there is a point in the world where everybody can change the world through his free individuality. When he observes and when he comes to a clear observation of facts he can work through these means. Now he stands in the culture and looks at other fields in the society and then he can see what is contained in the theory of an enlarged understanding of art growing and working through all power fields of the society. I would only stress this point, where there appears freedom in culture, where the outcome through active doings by free individuals with their self-conscious "I" is an amelioration, a bettering of the position of men in having consciousness of the whole problem, since now they are looking not only at the artist's problems but everybody's needs. There is also the question of equality in law in the society and the whole democratic power field. The idea of creativity is now flowing in this field, and one sees that creativity, these signs of freedom, and this declaration of art, which are related to a principle: the possibility to mold the world, to design the world, to sculpture the world, are not restricted to the problems of the artist. There is an anthropological determination of everybody's existence to be an artist in the society. Then one can see that the rule of structure, the formulation and the forming and the sculpturing of the constitution of the future has to go through free individuals and has to come from the grass roots in cooperation with all people together. Then one can see from this enlarged understanding of art that the battery of abilities, and therefore this society, which can be called an ability-society, could work and transform the whole power field of brotherhood, or the social field, or the until-now-called economical field. I say "until now," since this traditional idea of economy is still restricted by convention in the same way that traditional art is restricted.

But in enlarging this understanding of art, we are in the process of the totalization of the idea of art. We see that the totalization of art is now no longer related to the activities of artists and specialists in their insulated, isolated field of so-called cultural freedom. In reality this field is not free, it is only a free place where you can do what you want without rules and without responsibility. We can see that a totalized idea of art would ameliorate the possibilities in this field too. We see that the economical ideas are to be molded and sculptured according to this idea of totalized freedom, and that the totalized understanding of art totalizes the understanding of economy. No longer can the idea of production and enterprise be restricted in a field where only a physical production operates. All productions are now invested with the idea of a new anthropological declaration of human individual freedom and the enterprise which results from freedom. This is to declare that a spiritual being has therefore firstly the need for spiritual goods. By having these spiritual goods in a positive quality and by sculpturing the freedom field and the free field of cultural doings, the people will see that they have a need to organize only secondly all other needs, i.e., physical needs.

But the most important thing is to organize, and now appears the idea of organization as the idea of sculpture, as the idea of design, as the idea of molding and sculpturing the society. To regulate these processes, to have the means to regulate and to care for a structure in law necessitates a constitution. A law appears as a sculptural good of the people. It means it has to be done by the people. Therefore it now becomes a problem of basic questions. It will not be the practice of the future that only a minority with a special interest have the full political power to sculpture or to induce laws. And you will find that this law structure could work in the power field of economics, that there would be a law for the money, because the money is the most important sculpture as a regulating means of all creative processes. Since money regulates in all fields, in all the bloodstream of the society, it therefore has to have the character of a bloodstream. It has therefore to be described as a law-money, a bill of rights, while now it is only standing in a money-economics. The character of this money-economics will be metamorphized and will form an ability-society or spiritual-society.

I can only speak briefly and cannot expand on the whole score of complexities of such a view on the possibilities in society; I will only say that this stress on the free self-conscious "I" is not easy, is not comfortable. It asks for a lot of toughness, strong effort and continuous work. And therefore I will close this short speech, in which is implied my cordial thanks for what I received before, with the idea that there are only existing two possibilities, compulsion or making a sacrifice. In this sacrifice is implied the work of mankind in the future. Once more, only two alternatives exist, compulsion or sacrifice. In this way, in conclusion, I look back to the vision of John Milton, *Paradise Lost* and *Paradise Regained*.

ITS ELEMENTS

II

Interview with Kate Horsefield
1980

KATE HORSEFIELD: Were members of your family involved in any pursuit of creativity when you were a child?

JOSEPH BEUYS: No, I could never find out an interest in creativity. Perhaps there was one forefather from the Dutch roots of my family who was interested in science, but never could I find an interest in art.

HORSEFIELD: When you were a small child, did you have a direct interest in art?

BEUYS: No, this idea never came to my consciousness then, but if I look back, I find that what I did as a child had a lot to do with an understanding of art, from which I later developed this so-called "enlarged understanding of art" that has to do with the theory of Social Sculpture, the radical transformation of the world. So, what I did as a child—what I experienced in the fields, in nature and also in the industrial part of human activity, in small factories—had a kind of character which people can now see in the Guggenheim Museum pieces, for instance; but this is only apparent through a reflection about my interests as a child and the work I did then; and surely, not only what I did as a child, but also what I felt and what I thought, what I experienced and what . . . yes, imagined.

HORSEFIELD: Can you talk specifically about some of these particular kinds of feelings or experiences?

BEUYS: Yes—one of my most important general feelings during that time was that I felt myself, on one side, in a very beautiful environment; but from the side of social behavior, I felt that everything was in a very big debacle. I felt a dramatic contradiction in my life and when I was five years old, I felt that my life had to go to an end because I experienced already too much of this contradiction.

I had the feeling that another kind of life—perhaps in a transcendental area—would give me a better possibility to influence, or to work, or to act within this contradiction. So, this was my general feeling: on the one side, this beautiful undamaged nature from which I took a lot and had a lot of possibilities for contemplation, meditation, research, collecting things, making a kind of system; and on the other side, this social debacle that I felt already as a coming dilemma.

Yes, as a child I was aware of it, but later I could analyze the debacle. During my childhood, I was confronted with the nature of this behavior but didn't analyze the root of such a debacle; nevertheless, surely, this is an intuitive comprehension that already a child can feel; that in such a condition, the root must be in the behavior of the people.

You must see this as a very complicated thing insofar as I cannot accuse a single person to have been the cause of this debacle, this single person against me, and in no way do I intend to criticize certain people of my neighborhood in their behavior toward me. But I saw the relationship between people, I saw their thoughts, I saw their kind of expressionistic behavior in every difficult situation. I saw all the time the unclearness in the psychological condition of the people. You know, that was the time called the Roaring Twenties and I felt that this expressionistic behavior, this unformed quality of soul power and emotion of life . . . I saw it, that it would lead to a kind of catastrophe. That was my general feeling.

HORSEFIELD: Before you made the decision to be an artist, you were following some early interest in science and you had made up your mind to be a scientist to a certain extent . . .

BEUYS: That is true.

HORSEFIELD: What goals did you have as a scientist, and, then, what made you stop science and look more closely toward art?

BEUYS: Yes . . . I started from this positive point of the environment, where things in nature were undestroyed, relatively undestroyed, and I began already as a child to work with a sort of circus and theatrical methodology and system which were related to natural phenomena: animals, insects, plants.

When I was seven or eight, I got interested in research already done. I had teachers who were also close to this interest and I had a kind of laboratory all the time until fifteen years of age, when I developed really and factually a laboratory which was involved with physics, chemistry, zoology, botany and such things and I decided to study natural sciences. Then it was already near the time when the Second World War began and that activity was stopped by my call to military duty.

During the war, when I was a soldier, I had the privilege from my commander, when we were situated in a town where there was some academic activity, to go in my free time to the university. And since we had kind of a resting time in Poland, I had the opportunity to visit Poznan University. I think I had an event there, during a discussion with a professor of zoology about the whole theory of natural science, when I found out that this could not be my ability—to become so specialized in such a positivistic, materialistic field; these two terms came to my consciousness then, you know. It was a kind of methodology of the materialistic understanding of the world. So, I realized that the necessities of the so-called exact, natural sciences were a restriction for my specific ability and I decided to try it another way.

Then, during the rest of the war, I was pondering this problem. I had to make a decision about such established an understanding of research of the world and I had to think of a methodology to bring up my specific ability to cooperate with other people, simply to say . . . not to bring up very, very important things, that was not in my mind. In my mind was the question: how to cooperate with other people in a more meaningful way, to overcome not only the dilemma which I experienced in my youth already and from which the consequence was the Second World War—and this even stronger dilemma which I was mixed up in during the war. I thought about the necessity to come to a decision, to reconstruct, to renew the whole problem of life, labor, work of the people . . . Yes, this was for me the question after the crucial point of humankind's creativity and its implications: freedom of people in their creative work and how to develop from this necessity a kind of social order, another understanding of science and to try it with art. So—then—I tried it with art.

HORSEFIELD: One thing I'd like to ask is what was the art climate? What did you see about art as a field, you know, where could you attach your notions of experimentation, and what kind of goals could you have?

BEUYS: Yes, sure, it's a very important question because there was almost nothing to be seen, to be hopeful for in this field. The only hope I had was when I saw one day a photograph of a sculpture which was put away during Hitler's time. It was a sculpture by Wilhelm Lehmbruck, a German sculptor of expressionistic style. This was perhaps the only example, Lehmbruck, between my sixteenth to nineteenth years in which I saw a possibility for art to be principally of interest to innovate some things, instead of writing a very boring, naturalistic repetition of what is already done by nature.

That was a time, one must know, which was very isolated, generally, in Germany, during the fascist era and even more specifically isolated in that region where nobody was interested in art. That was a kind of tradition there, not because people were uncreative, but their professions were mostly agricultural and as far as the industrial impulse of the last century also had its traces in that area, they were workers, employed in factories. Within such a population, almost nothing existed culturally.

It was simply that they didn't know how to work in this specific field and also because of their involvement in the religious tradition—a Catholic area. So, when I saw such examples, one by Lehmbruck and also then some paintings, when I searched for interesting materials, I felt a possibility for art which would be better for my ability.

HORSEFIELD: At this point, were you studying art?

BEUYS: Yes.

HORSEFIELD: What kind of people were your teachers and how did they influence you at this time?

BEUYS: I started to prepare myself to enter a state academy. It was difficult during that time because all these institutions had been destroyed and they were all functioning in a kind of improvised roofing and only a few students could have the possibility to study. So, immediately after the war, after my time in prison, I began to work on some examples of what I felt could be a kind of proof of my skill, my ability, and with this stuff I went to the Academy of Düsseldorf and they took me, which was a wonder during that time. I, myself, was very astonished that they took me in this chaotic condition.

I started the university with a teacher who was very academic. I had nothing else to do than to copy models in a naturalistic, almost medical, way. He was pointing out to me where every muscle had to be, had to be observed, reproduced, and I made a lot of anatomic models until I felt very bored with this repetitive character of doing; and again I felt that it was a kind of science rather than art. I felt the parallelism with science and the influence that a materialistic understanding of it had on art. My professor appeared to me like a surgeon in a hospital with a white coat, and he had some tools in his breast pocket like a doctor when he came for correction. I felt like in an operating room, you know, and the work was exactly the same. I felt very upset and came in difficulties with this teacher who personally I loved very much because he was a generous person, a very noble character; but I came in difficulties and left him to try with another teacher.

This teacher, Ewald Mataré, was well-known during that time in the area. He had a style of his own, an understanding of art which was really a kind of innovation for me during that time. He had an autonomy in the understanding of art but with a medieval methodology. He was a believer in the *Bauhütte* idea, he was an admirer of the ornament, of what we call in Germany *Masswerk*, the geometrical . . . *Rechtfertigung, was heisst Recht-fertigung?* ["'Justification,' how do you say 'justification?'"] He was convinced that geometry and ornament should be the basis for all decisions in art. Then I was surely with a very good teacher, an autonomic character, but again I came in difficulties with such a dogma—with such a strict belief in an older concept of art coming from the Middle Ages, which brought me to a contradiction and discussion with him. He used to pay attention to my experiences with forms in different materials, and through his observation he declared me, simply, crazy. He didn't say that I was unable, no. He was saying that perhaps I was his most able student, but at the same time he felt it his duty to inform officials about the impossibility to take me later, for instance, as a teacher, because I was crazy—in his mind, completely crazy—a madman.

This was a time when I spoke a lot about the necessity to find a secure basis for further doings. I came to realize that it wouldn't lead to a solution of the problem to take, for instance, Buddhistic concepts, or Middle Ages *Bauhütte* concepts, or to take Tao things or other Eastern wisdom, to recreate spirituality within humankind. I was intensively involved with a kind of . . . yes, epistemology at that time and this was a reason for him to discard my work. He believed that an artist has to do the things, has not to speak too much, not to get so confused in such complicated stuff like historical analysis, and has not to brood upon these things. In his eyes I was a brooder, brooding on problems which humankind would never be able to solve, and from this point of view it appeared to him as a kind of madness.

It was already the beginning of my coming away from the traditional art world, getting more and more in connection with people who were interested in interdisciplinary research. And so I had more friends and more discussions with scientists again, and because I already had a scientific background and vocabulary, it was always a very intensive relationship with scientists of different fields. This is now the time from 1952 until the next point in my life—this point was a kind of break down of everything.

HORSEFIELD: Let me just insert one question before we go to that.

BEUYS: Yes, sure.

HORSEFIELD: To what extent were you interested in aesthetic solutions in the actual physicality of artmaking?

BEUYS: Say it again, please.

HORSEFIELD: To what extent were you interested in aesthetic solutions and in the process of making art?

BEUYS: Again, it's very important to understand the question and I didn't understand it clearly, therefore, please, say it again.

HORSEFIELD: O.K., as a contrast to art as a carrier of ideas, how interested in the aesthetics of solving a problem were you?

BEUYS: That was not a point at all for me. The word "aesthetics" does not exist for me. I found out during all my time in an official institution, a state academy, that this use of the word aesthetics meant nothing, in my understanding. I couldn't locate this meaning of aesthetics, which was a very nebulous, undetermined idea. I couldn't put it in any real and concrete way in my work, my problem, my view. But later, after what I said was the next period in my life, I stated my understanding of it: human being is aesthetics. Aesthetics is the human being in itself.

HORSEFIELD: You mentioned something earlier, before we started discussing your education as an artist, about being called into the war, during which period you were a pilot. I'd like to ask you about that time, and what were some of the incidents that happened to you, how they affected your concept of art as a social tool, and how it began to manifest itself in works of art?

BEUYS: Sometimes those things are looked at in a false way; these physical experiences during the war—accidents, damages on my body, wounds and such things—are overrated in regard to my later work.

HORSEFIELD: How were they overrated?

BEUYS: People look at it in too simplistic a way. They say that because I was in the war with Tataric tribes, for instance, and came in contact with these families—which took me in as a kind of family member to give me perhaps the possibility to desert the army, or when I was badly wounded such tribes found me and covered my body with a kind of fat, milky stuff—and even felt, that this would be the reason why I used such materials later in my work.

HORSEFIELD: Is that true?

BEUYS: True is this event during the war, but not true that that was the reason to take this stuff later for my sculpture. If this were true, then I ask why did I come so late to use such materials?

The proof of why this cannot be true, and is not true, is that before I did these things, I built up a theory to which these materials seemed the most appropriate, to make clear a theory of sculpture, a theory of social order, a theory of the action as a living sculpture and so on.

So, I came to elements, theoretical elements, of isolating materials, raw materials, organic materials. I didn't take these things just as a kind of immediately dramatical means because I was in a dramatic situation during the war, no, not at all; I wasn't interested in that. But later on, when I built up a theory and a system of sculpture and art and also a system of wider understanding—anthropological understanding of sculpture being related to the social body, and to everyone's lives and ability—then such materials seemed to be right and effectful tools to make clear this theory and to bring impulse in the discussion during the actions and the performances. But yes, surely, I remember the period of war, surely this time was very important for my whole life; and it is a very interesting point that the same material was involved in this emergency condition, personally and for the whole world during that war. So that was later also a very useful element to make clear how to overcome, one could say, the wound of all of us, not only mine. These elements appear as a kind of secret affinity in my life, but this relationship was not the motivation for me to use them.

HORSEFIELD: Would you say that these materials were chosen by you at a later time, developing out of your theory of sculpture?

BEUYS: Yes, you see they are clearly developed, and there were a lot of forerunners until I came to the simple decision to take such materials; and taking these materials, after my thoughts on the necessity of building a theory, I saw, then, the interesting relation they had to my biography.

HORSEFIELD: Were you surprised?

BEUYS: No, I wasn't surprised, because I told you already that during my childhood, I made such things instinctively, and from the creativity of a child, seeing the things in the same way as now. I worked with machines, one could say simply, that worked without fuel, without so-called physical energy, which would function with concepts. And now, I am slowly on the point to develop such machinery to work without physical energy, and as I can remember that already as a child I did the same thing; this made a significance in my life, that parallelism of past and future.

HORSEFIELD: How do you approach deciding to do a piece of art, or in certain case an action, what comes up to you before you start to do it? What do you know about it, and how do you proceed?

BEUYS: I know a lot before I start an action. I know a lot about the necessity of the general idea of sculpture, but I don't know anything about the process in which the action will run. When the action runs, my preparation works, because I am prepared to do a thing without knowing where it goes. You see, it would be a very uninteresting thing—it would have nothing to do with art— if it were not a new experiment for which I have no clear concept. If I had a clear concept of solving the problem, I would then speak about the concept and it wouldn't be necessary to make an action. Every action, every artwork for me, every physical scene, drawing on the blackboard, performance, brings a new element in the whole, an unknown area, an unknown world.

So, I never have a clear concept for a performance; I only make a decision about tools, for instance, but I don't determine the run of the action, or the character of the action at all. I never make actions to make actions, as a kind of innovation in the art world, as a new style. But I must say that the nature of the actions as a possibility to arrive at an understanding of art, for the most part was translated into an official modern art style and again became restricted to the enclosure of an ivory tower, reduced to a traditional view of art as a history of formal innovations without being seen as a possibility to innovate the whole social body. You see that is the dilemma in the art world—but I try to overcome that situation as much as I can; nevertheless, the problem always reappears, and I am always confronted with the temptation of the system to destroy such an impulse.

HORSEFIELD: I'd like to ask you in terms of people participating in your work, the audience for example, whether you want to refer to the audience at the actions, or the audience in Europe, or at the Guggenheim. A lot has been made out of the fact that people have to rely so much on verbal or written interpretations of your work in order to understand the symbols and the quality of the meaning behind it. This seems to me, in a way, to be a contradiction with the intention of reaching out across society.

BEUYS: If it were true, then it would be a contradiction, but you see, it isn't true. That is transported by a lot of unclear sources and unclear positions by people who are involved in this whole difficulty. Journalists, critics, and art historians, they are all building up this misunderstanding, that one must have interpretations for the phenomena of the production. It isn't true, simply it isn't true. People could work without interpretation, and they still can work without interpretation, but perhaps it is also interesting . . . Let's stop on this point, so as not to blur it out.

I never preserved a tool or a part of my laboratory, one could say, to avoid this term "artist". Because this is already an allusion to a kind of traditional understanding in a restricted way which wouldn't work on its own form, or the relationship between form, material and so on. Sometimes appears such a thing, and such a tool, which doesn't work without interpretation, but I would never give it as an example of my understanding of sculpture, or as a stimulating phenomenon to see something about the problems involved. So it is not necessary to have such an interpretation.

One of the most important statements of the enlarged understanding of art is that, not only materials—formed, or in chaos if necessary—has to do with sculpture. The thought is a sculptural process, and the expression of the thinking forms in language is also art. This totality of humankind's creativity—beginning with feelings and thoughts and their expression in a special material, the language material, for which you need your body and physical tools, your tongue, larynx, lungs, the air, the sound waves, the ear of the other person—all have to do with the idea of sculpture in the future.

There is on one side the physical consequence of the thought: the forms being realized in buildings, in architecture, in agricultural forms, in so-called sculptures because they have a special form; they imply a special imagination rather than being only a repetition of the given. It is possible for people to see those tools, the result of a process; they can see, one could say, the 'hardware' character of a process. But from this point we should look at the source, where the sculptural process starts, and it is the thought, the thinking power and its consequence, information, which means for me bringing form in material conditions.

Already when I speak I need my own body, the physical, flesh—it is a kind of clay to form into—and I need my lungs, I need my tools here, existing in my anatomy; I need the physical conditions of other forms of life, in my brother or my sister. I must at once eliminate discussions, interpretations, misunderstandings, deviations of the problem. I have to put everything in this process to bring up as much as possible the germ, the point of development in a special direction, to bring up a reasonable basis where new culture in the future could spring off.

So, that is the second part of the problem; that the language, the thinking on the problem is a more important sculpture even than the end of the process existing in tools or in paintings, or in drawings, or in carvings. This transcendent character of information, in an invisible world, gives us at the same time the proof and a clear knowledge that we are not only biological beings, material beings, but first spiritual beings, not existing on this planet— that we are only partly existing on this planet—and being involved in wood, in felt, in fat, in iron, in rubber or whatever resources of this planet.

That is for me the reason to speak, and it is the dignity of the speech. Otherwise, if this phenomenon, this reality, is not clear, then the consequence is that every speech is blah-blah, no social power exists, everything is chaos. And the other consequence is: let them do what they do, let the government do what it wants to do, I go out, I go apart and try to survive during my lifetime, and every language, every expression of human beings is blah-blah. If you don't find the necessity to speak, then surely the language is blah-blah. That is why I stress the necessity to find clear epistemological reasons to go on with art, which begin in humankind's thinking powers to mold, and to bring up the quality of what traditionally appears as the form of a thing, to impulse the world with a radical other understanding of culture.

In the past, it was the special spiritual authority of the high priest, the leader or the pharaoh or the tribal collective, the chief of the tribe, then later it was the capitalistic dependency on money power and state power, and now it has to deal with the world which is built up by people, people's creativity. But this will only be possible if people get slowly clear about the power they have, which starts in the thinking, the molding character of the thought. And the transference is in language forms and other kinds of language, as in the artwork where sculpture in its special physical form means also language—one must not have such a limited understanding of language.

That is for me the reason why I have to speak, and I have to speak more often than I do so-called artwork. You see, the complication is that I have to use something . . . I have to use a traditional determination for ideas, so when I speak about art, I can only say that there are two kinds of art: the traditional art, which is unable to bring up art at all, or to change anything in society or in the ability and the joy for life; and then, there is another kind of art, which is related to everybody's needs and the problems existing in society. This kind of art has to be worked out at the beginning; it has to start from the molding power of the thought as a sculptural means. If this sculptural agent is not active in the beginning, it will never lead to result in any physical form; or the physical form will only be pollution for the world and will only enrich the whole rubbish of production we already have. That is my meaning.

Interview with Willoughby Sharp
1969

WILLOUGHBY SHARP: Most of your catalog biographies state that you were born in Kleve, but you were actually born in Krefeld, weren't you?

JOSEPH BEUYS: Yes, I was born in a hospital in Krefeld, but that was purely accidental. My mother was making a short visit to Krefeld and I was born in the middle of it. But at most I spent three days there. I have no relationship to Krefeld, or more precisely to the landscape, but I do have a relationship to Kleve. That is where my parents always lived and where I grew up.

SHARP: How long did you live in Kleve?

BEUYS: Until 1961, when I was invited to be Professor at the Düsseldorf Art Academy.

SHARP: Then you attended school in Kleve?

BEUYS: Yes, all my schooling . . .

SHARP: Is there an art academy in Kleve?

BEUYS: No, I studied art in Düsseldorf. But I went to high school in Kleve until I became a soldier. At the end of 1947 I went to the Düsseldorf Art Academy and studied there until 1951. Then, after working for a while outside of Düsseldorf, I returned to Kleve.

SHARP: You worked in a studio?

BEUYS: Yes, I rented a small loft in an old bakery and I worked under the roof.

SHARP: Who did you study with at the Düsseldorf Art Academy?

BEUYS: Enseling and Mataré. Enseling was very academic, but Mataré was better. Mataré was very dogmatic but he raised issues that had to be considered. He thought that sculpture was basically ornamentation. This was a view to be contended with and, of course, we had great arguments. I had to reject his ideas, but nevertheless it was necessary for me to confront them. That's the way you learn as a student, and some of his ideas weren't totally uninteresting.

SHARP: That period must have been quite crazy. In 1951 much of Düsseldorf was still rubble and food was quite scarce. Was there any art then?

BEUYS: There was none at all.

SHARP: What about Lehmbruck?

BEUYS: Oh, Lehmbruck. He was a decisive figure during the war and I was very enthusiastic about some of his work. I once saw some Lehmbrucks in Kleve just before the war and they gave me my first real feeling for sculpture. But this was the only sculpture I was aware of at the time. Don't forget that I grew up in a small village during the Hitler period and I never saw any modern art.

SHARP: What about medieval or Renaissance sculpture?

BEUYS: Yes of course. I saw photographs of these things. But I didn't travel. I never got out of Kleve.

SHARP: You must have travelled as a soldier.

BEUYS: Yes, I took part in the whole war, from 1941 until 1946. I was in Russia.

SHARP: What did you see there?

BEUYS: Certainly not art! (*Laughs.*) What can I say? I was a fighter pilot. I cannot talk about the war. There were dead people lying around, everywhere.

SHARP: Were you in Stalingrad?

BEUYS: No, I was more to the south, in Ukraine, the Caucasus, Black Sea . . .

SHARP: And when the war ended?

BEUYS: During the last year of the war I was stranded on the Western front. There were no more planes, no more fuel. When peace was declared I became a British prisoner of war.

SHARP: Did the war influence your decision to become an artist?

BEUYS: Yes. Before the war I was a student of biology and mathematics, but this simply didn't satisfy me. You could say it was an emotional decision, but when you examine it a few years later you can begin to analyze it.

SHARP: Could you tell me more about what you did in the early fifties?

BEUYS: When I set up my own studio in Heerdt, a suburb of Düsseldorf, I was very friendly with the poet Adam Rainer Lynen. And I worked in that room until 1961 when I went back to Kleve.

SHARP: When did you become aware of Marcel Duchamp's work?

BEUYS: In 1955, I think.

SHARP: I feel the presence of Duchamp in one of your earliest pieces of sculpture, "Untitled," of 1954. Do you see any influence?

BEUYS: No, I don't think Duchamp influenced it at all. It was influenced by life. The open form is like a barracks window or ones you can see in old industrial cellars.

SHARP: So there's an architectural reference. What is the cylinder in front of the open chamber?

BEUYS: It's a steel gas container covered with plaster.

SHARP: None of your works have bases?

BEUYS: Bases used to annoy me, even when I was in the Academy. They are only an auxiliary means to help things stand up. They are like an artificial lawn. Just after I finished my first figures, I removed them from their bases because they disturbed me so much. It was only later that I recognized the base as an important sculptural element, perhaps the most important element. There are some sculptures that consist of nothing but a base.

SHARP: A work in which the base is irrelevant is your "The Needles of a Christmas Tree," of 1962.

BEUYS: That's true. This is a Christmas tree that stood around here for two years. Eventually it lost all its needles and they lie all around it.

SHARP: You moved to the Drakeplatz studio in March 1961, so this was your first Christmas tree here. Did you always see it as a sculpture?

BEUYS: Yes, I saw its beauty. But it's not only beautiful, it's also ugly. You may say a Christmas tree with needles is beautiful and one without needles is ugly. No, I wanted to have it, and we did, for a long time, until the worms destroyed it.

SHARP: Oh. . . .

BEUYS: Two years ago I created a political party for animals.

SHARP: Do you have a lot of animals in the party?

BEUYS: It's the largest party in the world.

SHARP: And you are the leader?

BEUYS: I am the leader.

SHARP: You're crazy. (*Laughter.*)

BEUYS: And therefore I am a very mighty man. Mightier than Nixon. (*More laughter.*)

SHARP: But he has all the insects.

BEUYS: I have all the insects.

SHARP: They are not animals.

BEUYS: Insects are animals.

SHARP: Where does the fat come in? To attract the flies into the party?

BEUYS: The fat is in the room, the party's meeting room (*laughter*). To make things clearer, let me give you this statement concerning "The Art Pill" (1963): Vehicle Art:

The Chief of the Stags could plug anywhere into the environment, whether on the inside of a room with flat, curved or chaotic surfaces. Yes, even amorphous rooms gave him the energy to bake his cakes. He didn't despair when at first he succeeded in producing only flat, unseemly pancakes which shriveled up in the pan. On the contrary, he was encouraged in his determination since he had not lost faith in the effectiveness of "The Art Pill." Nevertheless, some salutory by-products resulted from his activity, namely art to be rubbed in, art taking the form of a salve, art in the form of a sausage, art to be cut into slices.

SHARP: I assume, then, that you are the Chief of the animals and that this can be seen in your work. "The Chief," of 1963–4, which you performed rolled up in a felt rug with a dead hare at each end and fat works in the corners of the room.

BEUYS: Yes, I speak for the hares that cannot speak for themselves.

SHARP: Which you do literally by making noises which are amplified in the room and in the street.

BEUYS: The human responsibility to all living things . . .

SHARP: I remember that you met Bob Morris in Düsseldorf before his Schmela Gallery show in the fall of 1964.

BEUYS: Morris visited me. I showed him all my works. I wanted to do "The Chief" with him. We arranged to do the work simultaneously. We wanted to start at the same second and then work for nine hours, me in Berlin, he in New York.

SHARP: Did you do it?

BEUYS: Yes, I did it in Berlin, but he didn't do it.

SHARP: Why not?

BEUYS: I don't know, but he didn't do it. He left Düsseldorf after his show. I wrote everything down for him. I drew a sketch with the dimensions, gave him all the instructions with regard to space and all the elements involved.

SHARP: There seems to be some similarity in sensibility between "The Chief" and some of Morris' theatrical works, but I can understand why he might not have wanted to do it. (*At this point Beuys drew my attention to some photos of his* "Fettecke" *or* "Fat Corner.") There must be a lot of action in these works for you. [Beuys called these works *"Aktionen."*] You did some *"Fettecken"* as part of "The Chief," didn't you?

BEUYS: Yes, (*points to the photo of* "The Chief," 1964). Here is one. It is a transmitter, and I am also a transmitter. Both are sculptural elements. That is a very important concept for me. If I produce something, I transmit a message to someone else. The origin of the flow of information comes not from matter, but from the "I," from an idea. Here is the borderline between physics and metaphysics: this is what interests me about this theory of sculpture. Take a hare running from one corner of a room to another. I think this hare can achieve more for the political development of the world than a human being. By that I mean that some of the elementary strength of animals should be added to the positivist thinking which is prevalent today. I would like to elevate the status of animals to that of humans.

SHARP: Your "Iron Coffer Containing 100 Kilos of Fat and 100 Dismantled Air Pumps," 1968, is a part of the *"Fettecken"* series.

BEUYS: It is the final stage of the action. One that incorporates a very complex array of concepts. The iron coffer in the form of one half of a cross stands in the center of a cellar. It is a piece of sculpture which contains both fat and air pumps. The fat embodies mass, the positive principle, and the air pumps represent a vacuum, a negative principle. All the air pumps are broken. A letter is nailed outside the box indicating its contents: 100 kilos of fat, 100 air pumps.

   (*Then Beuys points abruptly to another photograph.*) "Set III" is composed of nine equal elements made of layers of felt topped by a rectangular plate of copper of the same size. They have a relationship to the room which is hard to define. They fill the space, but I am not interested in the physical aspect of filling. I want the work to become an energy center, like an atomic station. It's the same principle again: transmitter and receiver. The receiver is the same as the transmitter, only in felt. It is a totalization. The spectator becomes the program. The spectator, represented by the felt, equals the program. An identification of transmitter and receiver.

   Actually two elements, fat and felt, are closely related. Both have a homogeneous character in that they have no inner structure. Felt is a material pressed together, an amorphous material, with an uneven structure. The same is true of the nature of fat, and that interested me. But there is also the element of the

filter—and I worked with gauze filters before I worked with fat—
and there is an element of isolation in it.

SHARP: There also is a minimal element in your work, especially
"Set III" and "Felt Corner," 1963.

BEUYS: Yes, the idea of minimal is expressed in these works, but
they are not minimal art. It's different. It overlaps. It's minimal,
but in the sense of something very reduced. But there is no direct
connection in my work to minimal art.

SHARP: Has your teaching at the Düsseldorf Art Academy for the
last eight years been an important function for you?

BEUYS: It's my most important function. To be a teacher is my
greatest work of art. The rest is the waste product, a demonstra-
tion. If you want to explain yourself you must present something
tangible. But after a while this has only the function of a historic
document. Objects aren't very important for me anymore. I want
to get to the origin of matter, to the thought behind it. Thought,
speech, communication—and not only in the socialist sense of
the word—are all expressions of the free human being.

SHARP: Would you say then that your goal is to make man freer
and stimulate him to think more freely?

BEUYS: Yes, I am aware that my art cannot be understood primarily by thinking. My art touches people who are in tune with my
mode of thinking. But it is clear that people cannot understand
my art by intellectual processes alone, because no art can be
experienced in this way. I say to experience, because this is not
equivalent to thinking: it's a great deal more complex: it involves
being moved subconsciously. Either they say, "Yes, I'm in-

terested," or they react angrily and destroy my work and curse it. In any event I feel I am successful, because people have been affected by my art. I touch people, and this is important. In our times, thinking has become so positivist that people only appreciate what can be controlled by reason, what can be used, what furthers your career. The need for questions that go beyond that has pretty much died out of our culture. Because most people think in materialistic terms they cannot understand my work. This is why I feel it's necessary to present something more than mere objects. By doing that people may begin to understand man is not only a rational being.

SHARP: What can a sculptor do in this situation?

BEUYS: Sculpture must always obstinately question the basic premises of the prevailing culture. This is the function of all art, which society is always trying to suppress. But it's impossible to suppress it. Now, even politicians are becoming aware of that. Art—its new concepts, schools, even revolutionary groups—now has a strong vitality throughout the world. Slowly people are beginning to realize that the creative spirit cannot be subdued.

SHARP: Then you see the artist as a provocateur?

BEUYS: Provocateur—that's it exactly. To provoke means to evoke something. By making a sculpture with fat or a piece of clay I evoke something. I ignite a thought within me—a totally original, totally new thought that has never yet existed in history, even if I deal with a historical fact or with Leonardo or Rembrandt. I myself determine history—it is not history that determines me. Economic circumstances do not determine me. I determine them. Every man is a potential provocateur.

SHARP: How does art improve life?

BEUYS: Art alone makes life possible—this is how radically I should like to formulate it. I would say that without art man is inconceivable in physiological terms. There is a certain material-ist doctrine which claims that we can dispense with mind and with art because man is just a more or less highly developed mechanism governed by chemical processes. I would say man does not consist only of chemical processes, but also of metaphys-ical occurrences. The provocateur of the chemical processes is located outside the world. Man is only truly alive when he realizes he is a creative, artistic being. I demand an artistic involvement in all realms of life. At the moment art is taught as a special field which demands the production of documents in the form of artworks. Whereas I advocate an aesthetic involvement from science, from economics, from politics, from religion— every sphere of human activity. Even the act of peeling a potato can be a work of art if it is a conscious act.

SHARP: Which artists do you feel close to?

BEUYS: John Cage. These concepts are not alien to him.

SHARP: What about the new Italian sculptors like Mario Merz or American sculptors like Richard Serra?

BEUYS: Yes, I feel close to them, because they are contempo-raries. But not that close because I have a feeling that these things have already been done. Perhaps the reason I love Cage and Nam June Paik more is because they are at the point of origin. Things have a certain reach. Beyond that everything is derivative. From that point of view most of the works at Bern

("When Attitudes Become Form") were late works. I have been doing these things for a long time, and now I am questioning their value.

SHARP: What do you think of the work of Mike Heizer, Dennis Oppenheim, Robert Smithson, and Keith Sonnier?

BEUYS: I don't know their work that well, but I spoke to Bruce Nauman at Bern.

SHARP: Nauman's work shares a similar sensibility.

BEUYS: Yes, but I find it hard to define because I don't know Nauman's inner intentions. I place great importance on inner intentions. I don't know anything about Nauman's thought processes, but I can say that his works look closer to my art than any other works do.

SHARP: Then you don't often come into contact with the works of other artists?

BEUYS: I rarely go to exhibitions, and I hardly ever read art journals. If I happen to see one, I look at it, but my interest is not so great that I follow these things daily. I am more interested in the development of thoughts . . . I am not at all interested in whether other people use elements of my work.

SHARP: Do you feel the same about Morris?

BEUYS: Yes, but I was a bit surprised when Morris started working with felt. But I couldn't say more. Last year Morris invited me to participate in an exhibition he was arranging. But I couldn't do it.

SHARP: The Castelli Warehouse Exhibition in New York?

BEUYS: Yes.

SHARP: Why didn't you participate?

BEUYS: I didn't think it was necessary.

SHARP: Didn't you have any work?

BEUYS: No, I didn't have anything at the time that I could have given away. Karl Ströher had just bought all my works (about three hundred) but I guess I could have made something for it. I just didn't feel like it. Later some people told me it was a good thing I didn't participate, because the exhibition wasn't really all that good.

SHARP: That's not true. It was one of the best shows of the year.

BEUYS: All right. Then it was a mistake that I didn't send anything, but one cannot do everything.

SHARP: I see you have a great reluctance to do exhibitions.

BEUYS: Yes, I was always extremely reluctant, because for me an exhibition is something that is already dead. It is something I only allow myself to be forced to do. I will only do an exhibition when there is absolutely no way out. . . .

SHARP: That explains why you have only shown two or three times during your ten-year association with Alfred Schmela.

BEUYS: Yes, I keep on refusing to exhibit until someone like Schmela convinces me that it's an absolute necessity.

SHARP: Is this a reaction against materialism in general, or is it due to the fact that there are more demands on you today than there were in 1967?

BEUYS: Both. People are becoming more demanding. They are getting sharper. I was glad when Ströher took everything away. Things have to be some place, and I have never wanted to collect my own things. I like empty walls best.

SHARP: You've been working for twenty years, and it's only recently that people have begun to appreciate what you have accomplished.

BEUYS: This is a fairly recent development. For ten or fifteen years people mocked me and said, "Beuys is crazy."

SHARP: Yes, I remember when I first visited Düsseldorf in 1957 no one except one or two artists defended you. Things have changed now. What do you think about your present situation within the context of art?

BEUYS: I think the crux of the matter is that my work is permeated with thoughts that do not originate in the official development of art but in scientific concepts. You know, to begin with I wanted to be a scientist. But I found that the theoretical structure of the natural sciences was too positivist for me, so I tried to do something new for both science and art. I wanted to widen both areas. So as a sculptor I tried to broaden the concept of art. The logic of my art depends on the fact that I have had one idea which I have obstinately worked with. Actually it's a problem of perception.

SHARP: Perception?

BEUYS: (*After a long hesitation.*) In the simplest terms, I am trying to reaffirm the concept of art and creativity in the face of Marxist doctrine. The socialist movements in Europe which are now strongly supported by the young constantly provoke this question. They define man exclusively as a social being. I wasn't surprised by this development, which led to the confused political conditions, not only in Germany but also in America.

Man really is not free in many respects. He is dependent on his social circumstances, but he is free in his thinking, and here is the point of origin of sculpture. For me, the formation of the thought is already sculpture. The thought is sculpture. Of course, language is sculpture. I move my larynx. I move my mouth and the sound is an elementary form of sculpture. Man hasn't thought much until now about sculpture. We ask: "What is sculpture?" And reply: "Sculpture." The fact that sculpture is a very complex creation has been neglected. What interests me is the fact that sculpture supplies a definition of man.

SHARP: Isn't that rather abstract?

BEUYS: My theory depends on the fact that every human being is an artist. I have to encounter him when he is free, when he is thinking. Of course, thinking is an abstract way of putting it. But these concepts—thinking, feeling, wanting—are concerned with sculpture. Thought is represented by form; feeling by motion or rhythm; will by chaotic force. This explains the underlying principle of my *"Fettecke."* Fat in liquid form distributes itself chaotically in an undifferentiated fashion until it collects in a differentiated form in a corner. Then it goes from the chaotic principle to the form principle, from will to thinking. These are parallel concepts which correspond to the emotions, to what could be called soul.

SHARP: Is it difficult to decide to execute a work now?

BEUYS: Humm ... The question is if it is important to make sculpture now. I often question the necessity of doing it. The more I consider the problem, the more I think that there's only a few things that I need to make. I want to try to only do those that have some importance. I have no interest in production as such. I am neither interested in making works for commerce nor for the pure pleasure of seeing them. It is getting much harder to make things. But one is forced to translate thought into action and action into object. The physicist can think about the theory of atoms or about physical theory in general. But to advance his theories he has to build models, tangible systems. He too has to transfer his thought into action, and the action into an object. I am not a teacher who tells his students only to think. I say act; do something: I ask for a result. It may take different forms. It can have the form of sound, or someone can do a book, make a drawing or a sculpture. I don't care. Although I am a Professor of Sculpture at the Düsseldorf Art Academy, I accept all forms of creativity.

SHARP: How do you think future historians will judge your contribution to art?

BEUYS: I am not at all interested in being placed on a value scale—almost as good as Rembrandt, as good as Rubens or Goya. After I am dead I would like people to say, "Beuys understood the historical situation. He altered the course of events." I hope, in the right direction.

"Time's Thermic Machine"
a public dialogue, Bonn
1982

JOSEPH BEUYS: . . . Oak trees had a specific role to play not only during the Nazi period but even before then in the Wilhelmina era: it is certainly possible to misuse all these traditions, but even when abused, they do reveal another kind of factor; and that is the polarity between the culture of the North and that of the South. Once again, under the sign of the oak, flowers the ancient contrast between the decentralized, almost barbarous culture of the Germanic peoples and the Celts, and the Latin conscience of urban character. The decentralized, itinerant and nomadic element in the Celtic and Germanic nature is today current once again.

It will naturally now be possible to prevent there being initiated any manipulation intent on opening the way to a historical and regressive conquest of a barbarous and inhumane past. We, on the contrary, intend with a new production of organic architecture to take action devoted to the future. We are perfectly aware that the most remote past and the most distant future come together under this sign.

BERNHARD BLUME: You quoted precisely the tradition which views the oak as a symbol whose roots reach back to the most remote—and I would add mythical—past. We know that the oak in Germanic lands was the sacred tree, the tree of Thor, the god of thunder and lightning. Unless I'm mistaken, wasn't the tree also the symbol of justice—its strong boughs supported men put to death. And since it is a tree which grows either on the edge of woods or right out in open fields, it could symbolize the power of nature. Furthermore, I believe the incarnation of the oak together with the forces of nature already occurred in mythical times. The ideological manipulation took place only later, in the nineteenth and twentieth centuries.

BEUYS: First of all it is not true that we are responsible for these connections. This tree, which according to the religious customs of the Germans and Celts functioned as a fulcrum for any spiritual action, spread in the form of a Celtic tree, from Turkey to as far as Scotland and Ireland; that is to say across entire Europe and certainly to a greater extent in the southern areas. Meanwhile in northern Europe the Germanic peoples have also singled out the oak as the point for holding meetings. The oak has a specific role for the Britannic people; for a people, that is, who are our blood relations. For them it is the tree of the Druids. The word "Druid" means oak.

AUDIENCE: Having concluded your historical summary of the oak, what is the new element in your plan?

BEUYS: I touched upon it in the beginning when I spoke of a new cultural shell which will embrace the earth. The biosphere, as a healthy, biological and essential atmosphere consistent with human needs, will naturally also play a part in this shell, in this new enveloping nature; but in saying this we certainly do not mean to say that the process will finish there: we must continue along the road of interrelating socio-ecologically all the forces present in our society until we perform an intellectual action which extends to the fields of culture, economy and democratic rights.

It is a question therefore of developing a new concept of capital which takes into account before all else the inner needs of man. At this point, however, our inner needs appear once again to be in strict relation with what the ancient cultures have expressed about them: in other words understood, let us say, as a spiritual action and one which was manifested in the Druids in a manner opposite to that of the ancient mystery priests, for example. Hence the past supports the future in a single picture. It is marvellous to think that man today is able to personify simultaneously both past and future and can draw from it substance which is immeasurably greater than anything humanity could have had in the past; and man can do this with only a little effort on his part.

AUDIENCE: But why specially the oak and not other trees?

BEUYS: No, that's not the problem! I've already spoken before about trees! I really didn't want to act in an arbitrary manner. I wanted a tree capable of provoking all these questions. Locust trees, for example, could not have conjured up any kind of associations concerning religious, spiritual or historical questions. The locust tree (*robinia pseudoacacia*) has grown in our country in mixed woods since the Ice Age. It has never had, however, any specific significance. Therefore we had to find a tree which could bear all these problems and we didn't want to be dogmatic about it. In other words, we didn't want to plant it where it couldn't have grown! Let's forget plane trees then, and those which adapt themselves in one way or another to certain urban situations, like, for example, the ginkgo, a living fossil which has survived all the natural disasters which have befallen the world from the Ice Age and the Cretaceous period to our own times. The ginkgo is like that, and we'll plant that too!

AUDIENCE: But why the oak in particular? It seems to me that the oak could easily be suspected of Germanism and of a German past with connotations of nationalism. Had ginkgo been adopted, it would have been a better symbol: the ability to survive all catastrophes and as a projection towards the future.

BEUYS: We really ought to quash this so-called "German question," but we must resolve it once and for all. It is similar above all else to the problem felt by many people in a fundamental, spiritual form. I have already stated that it is not the Germans who have availed themselves most of the oak, but rather the Celts, that is to say a people who were living principally in France; there the oak grows rather better than it does in Germany whose climate is harsher. It also grows well in the British Isles which enjoy a maritime climate and are warmed by the Gulf Stream. There, that's what we want to do—to create time's thermic machine, something different then from the methods of some mysticism of the past based on a misunderstood Germanism.

Blume shows several illustrations of trees made by a Mormon.

BEUYS: The Mormon naturally didn't know anything about trees! They're neither oaks nor beeches but rather gigantic trees with leaves like those of a lilac! He really didn't understand anything! (*laughter*) He only wanted to have beams which seemed like trees! (*laughter*)

AUDIENCE: Can we hope that in fifty or a hundred years trees will still exist?

BEUYS: Optimism has really nothing to do with what is necessary! Our actions must be based neither on optimism nor pessimism. If we allowed ourselves to be influenced by these impulses, dictated by feelings which conjure up either like or dislike, we wouldn't be able to do anything sensible anymore. On Blume's badge there is even written: "Pure reason is green!" That's it! It means that we can't allow ourselves to be guided by like and dislike: we must only be guided by what the situation requires. Then we can expect—we don't want to hope at all—that man in fifty years' time will have a relationship with nature which is fifty percent or 100 percent better than at present, and so on in a hundred or two hundred years' time. And all this is precisely because we consider the tree to be alive, just as we may consider the human conscience to be growing and its source to be the human spirit. We expect this of ourselves and of humanity! This means that it's not a case of hoping, believing or doubting but rather realizing that something must be made which is a real creation. If this creation is destroyed by other men, then a historical process will be concluded from which will spring yet another.

AUDIENCE: Don't you think that the pollution of the environment and its progressive increase will compromise the organic life of the trees in fifty years' time?

BEUYS: Here's Bernhard again!

Blume reads some pages of Global 2000 *dedicated to "trees and woods." Afterwards, Blume suggests one of the possible ways of recovering our arboreal heritage: for example, constructing furniture with old wooden planks as he himself does.*

BEUYS: Now, that's an excellent idea: even without planting trees we can at least retain intact our arboreal heritage: for example, I save at least one tree every month by keeping all the paper I use, which is then collected every month by a group of boys from Düsseldorf. This paper will be recycled to make cardboard! We don't need to cut down a tree to make cardboard! If families reorganized themselves into producers of raw materials—and it wouldn't be all that difficult—the entire economic process would be rapidly restructured. It would most certainly aid the conservation of nature if people left newspapers in containers which would then be removed every month or fortnight to be reinserted into the natural cycle. Instead of this, newspapers are thrown onto any rubbish pile, where they perhaps contaminate underground water courses, because they rot and produce substances which are harmful to the ecological balance.

BLUME: We're not professional ecologists but we're working towards a noble and cultural enterprise. We can create monuments which go far beyond fine appearances: then having children won't be so senseless as it is at the moment.

BEUYS: It's obvious that children who grow up in a place where there are flowers and trees and where the air is filtered by the respiratory processes of these creatures, develop vital strengths rather different from those children who don't experience this change. For this reason I don't entirely agree with Blume when he states that the artist or art are not able to develop a professional approach to ecology. I believe, however, that the concept of professionalism must be considered separately. Indeed, if by "professional" we mean the capacity to evaluate a detail deduced from a general problem, then I agree that a science of that kind should exist. This type of science coincided with the birth of science in general. However, it has been proved that precisely this scientific professionalism has destroyed the earth and human well-being.

For this reason we believe that only art can develop that highly ordered professionalism needed to overcome individual specialization in the fields of biology, forestry and dendrology, which are the branches which deal with the range of problems concerning trees. This is true also of the branch of chemistry which utilizes cellulose. This is why we believe that a well-ordered idea of ecology and professionalism can stem only from art—art in the sense of the sole, revolutionary force capable of transforming the earth, humanity, the social order, etc. This is because at the moment none of history's developments, including those regarding the notion of exact science, have been capable of facing this fundamental problem. Art is, then, a genuinely human medium for revolutionary change in the sense of completing the transformation from a sick world to a healthy one. In my opinion, only art is capable of doing it. After all the experiments like those done in the past at Kassel it is logical that at a certain point we also abandon the physical edifice which represents so to speak the "modern" and turn instead to the spot where men at their place of work and in their homes represent the basis of this expanded concept of art. This means that every man is an artist or must be considered as such since man's creativity is the real capital of a society. Following this argument, capitalism and communism, both retrograde and antiquated concept of capital, must be transformed into a notion which firmly recognizes that humanity's real capital consists of human capacity.

AUDIENCE: I wonder how politics could possibly affect monuments and art. Planting oak trees is certainly fine but will the politicians then make laws saying more trees must be planted? How can politics possibly affect art?

BEUYS: It's true that the problems can't be solved by simply planting seven thousand oak trees. Appropriate associations must be linked to this action, to this symbolic act, to this creature-tree, and it's precisely these that we are speaking of now. We have stated that these vital economic laws must exist in the same form as we demand them now and must be capable of changing the state of emergency in which humanity finds itself into something better. To sum up, I have spoken of the following progressive plan of action: ORGANIZATION FOR DIRECT DEMOCRACY-FREE INTER-NATIONAL UNIVERSITY—necessity of revolutions—anticipation of a society to the point where men today require economic laws which are universally valid as, say, active measures. Besides, the legislator in ancient cultures was the Druid—the legislator who stood under the oak tree. Here the oak appears once again as architecture, itinerant and decentralized, and which deals with these new questions and vitally important ideas not only so as to form a monument of an aesthetic king but above all to place the necessity of the new economic concept at the center of man's thought.

BLUME: Until now economic reason has never been rational: at most it has been rationally functional. This notion needs yet to be completed. Reason, as it has been developed by the bourgeoisie into a society with a capitalist economy, and as it has been philosophically supported by Emmanuel Kant, is an administrative reason which cannot only aim at its own reformation but must also become more moral. It must be greener!—not rationality based merely on calculation, but rather one which is binding and responsible.

AUDIENCE: But I'm still wondering how all this can be politically imposed.

BEUYS: By working with the Greens!

AUDIENCE: Isn't it perhaps simplistic to say, "by working with the Greens?"

BEUYS: Not at all! If you participated in the practical work of the Greens, you would see that they are extremely well-versed people whatever their level of ability—we're interested in everything from alternative sources of energy to gnosiology. However naive this comment may seem, if we consider it from the point of view of party politics, in the sense of the old political militancy (which not even I believe in), it is no other than a suggestion to try to take an individual, political path to solve this problem which regards the expansion of the conscience, the true conscience in action. This must be said! On some occasions, when talking on the subject of trees, I have pointed to the importance of a new conscience, especially because conscience is a necessity for man himself in the sense of an anthropological essence which does not know itself nor its own strengths. And here we are straight away into the development of the conscience: What exactly is man? Whatever has he in common with the oak? In what way is the oak superior to him? In short, where is the affinity between man and oak? The answer is naturally that which flows also in his bones and his organs: that is to say that man is a creature like the oak! But what do we mean by life? And what exactly is that docility which runs through our lives? Is it similar to that possessed by both men and animals? What is conscience of that which is life and adaptability and that which makes man superior to an animal? The answer is that it is the normal conscience which in history is fulfilled at different levels: it is that conscience of the ego which invests human freedom in our own times and from which it is necessary to demand man's self-determination in all his working activities by means of political decisions! This is material regarding the conscience material which we find in the Greens, in the men reunited under the name of the Greens.

This is radically different from what is discussed in conventional political parties.

AUDIENCE: Mr. Beuys, as far as I understand, you want to plant oak trees at Kassel.

AUDIENCE: Not only at Kassel!

BEUYS: Yes, first of all at Kassel: the symbolic re-forestation of the earth will begin at Kassel!

AUDIENCE: Even if the area around Kassel is deforested in order to construct the new western runway, Assia is still the most wooded region of West Germany. Don't you think it would be rather more effective—and more in the spirit of the Greens—if these trees were planted in the Sahel belt or perhaps in South America? I'm sure you would be able to carry out this project in practice.

BEUYS: Yes, it is possible . . . slowly though. The thing doesn't really work like that.

AUDIENCE: But why exactly at Kassel?

BEUYS: In the first place it is an area where technology is highly developed and from where the greatest damage is spread to the world. Following this first break, from where the initial steps in the transformation of the conscience will stem, we will naturally take action in the areas where this reafforestation would be more important: for example, as you have said, in the Sahel.

AUDIENCE: Mr. Beuys . . .

BEUYS: Please let me finish. It's for this reason that we don't want to say: there are seven thousand oaks. It's more a question of the entrepreneurial character of a judicious action: planting trees in the Sahel area. We are waiting to be assigned the task! However, we have to prepare the ground in order that it can be planned and carried out rationally. For instance, if I go to the Sahel area, dig a hole and plant something, the day after it'll be all dried up, unless it is done in a particular way. First it is necessary to create a rational, organizational net: this way these vital processes can develop in the various locations—when the case presents itself—with a certain coherency. It could happen that tomorrow I'll receive from Argentina the job of planting trees in the Falkland Islands—that would solve the problem!

AUDIENCE: There exists the proverb "To take coals to Newcastle." Perhaps in the future people will say: "To take oaks to Kassel."

BLUME: It's a fact though that where there are oaks the climate is certainly better.

BEUYS: Absolutely right!

BLUME: . . . in the Sahel area as well! And the chances that they grow better in Kassel are greater because, even if the wind always blows from the west, where West Germany perhaps . . .

BEUYS: . . . it is just a place where something international is happening! The effect of an international undertaking like this with such a hold on universal consciousness, will be seen for itself. A center better than this one, where, with relatively exiguous means (seven thousand oaks are expensive without a doubt, but as means are still fairly exiguous), and where it is possible to propagate something like this in the world, does not exist. Planted around one hotel, the Holiday Inn, there are sixty oaks! First of all, sooner or later the Holiday Inn will give me back the money spent on the sixty oak trees, and then will circulate this letter in all its sixteen hundred hotels throughout the world. *(Beuys shows the F.I.U./Dia Art Foundation circular which is a sort of invitation to join.)*

In this way it will be there, in every room! Each hotel has at least three hundred bedrooms, there are sixteen hundred Holiday Inns throughout the Middle East, Australia, America and South America, and they will all be proposing this splendid idea!

BLUME: What is more, every four or five years Kassel becomes a hot international point. Who meets there? The cream of international culture who, with the economic system they have, contribute towards progressive deforestation. Thus it takes on a symbolic function.

AUDIENCE: I'd like to say something about the Green Party. They do not have the majority in the Bundestag at this moment.

When they do it may well be too late. How do you think of concretely influencing the current parties to give a practical turn to your work? It seems to me to be still a little theoretical.

BEUYS: I am not at all for influencing parties and politicians.

AUDIENCE: But they are the ones who make the laws!

BEUYS: It won't be very long before they will not be able to make these laws. Humanity will not put up with these senseless laws for long. We work along these lines as best we can. We do, however, know that we are confronted with a power consolidated in its historical experience. We can oppose this with only a much smaller one—and this is easy to admit. Pure reason, as it happens, is green! Didn't Blume write that, in the paper? I hope you are not thinking that we are suddenly going to be able to change this life and its social relationships overnight. As Rudi Dutschke said, after the long march through the institutions, after long stages of political fight, one day we shall make laws as men. At that moment I shall have been dead for quite some time. Those men that are called the Green Party today will have another name in twenty to thirty years from now. These sensible men will be able to make these laws as the Druid, the lawgiver, made his laws under the oak of ancient times.

FRANZ DAHLEM: You can say that politicians "watering" themselves now become "blue." Who knows if, in a short time, they won't turn green?

BEUYS: Precisely!

AUDIENCE: Well said!

BLUME: In short, pure reason is green. Let us not say that it is so everywhere, but that it will be soon.

(Here follows a brief talk by Blume on "reason.")

BEUYS: On the question we are dealing with one can also say something that is simple—let us try to touch the extreme! And let us do it, according to possibility, on the basis of your points of view. We know very well that the Greens themselves, of whom I am one, do not know the problem in all its complexity. They haven't arrived at the definitive form of the problem. We know very well that the Green problem is something that develops over time. We would be in a much better situation though, if you were to participate actively in the Green movement. Indeed your creativity, in fact, contributes to the general creative circulation, and this is what we need.

BLUME: Recently I learnt that consciousness is in a growing phase, even with the politicians, who worked in quite another way before. Franz Dahlem tells me that he has some seventy newspaper cuttings with pictures of politicians letting themselves be photographed in the act of planting trees. There was a time when children were the symbol of the future. All this is ridiculous. Let us hope that the consciousness of the management that has got us to this point stays quiet. This is the objective of our work. It is presented in quite a concrete way, and there are small steps forward such as our little poster here.

BEUYS: Yet it is also important to be able to talk about politicians and use different terms from those in common use. They are *politicians* precisely because they are in an encrusted shell-like structure by now devoid of any vitality. But they *are* like us. Suffice it to say that when that ancient power wanes these men will come together in this Green movement. Any loss of power can also be positive for the future. We shall contribute actively in paring away this shell-structure and towards the development of a new condition. All this will happen *with* these men that we call politicians and not *against* them! Against the structure, yes. It is that which makes us call these men politicians, within it as they are, and knowing, as it does, the concept of "politics" above all—complicity between the power of money and the power of the state. The summing up is quickly done. There will have to be no more politics!

And at the moment in which they no longer exist, these men, in their own ambits, will form a sensible society. They will have reached the *formal concept* we intend. We hold that politics should be substituted by the formal concept since all the problems of life, even the organization of world economy, are nothing less than problems relative to their appropriate *forms.* From the moment when you realize what this gigantic social work of art is, when new social orders are understood, you are freed from those arguable concepts of "politics" and "politicians" and able to consider men in their most varied forms of action as just that—men.

BLUME: Then move on to the sale of the "Tree Fund" posters.

BEUYS: Thank you for your attention and for such informed participation, not to mention the contribution for the trees.

AUDIENCE: Jawohl!

Interview with Richard Demarco
1982

RICHARD DEMARCO: Your exhibition at the Anthony d'Offay Gallery strikes a somber note underlined by the title: *"Dernière Espace avec Introspecteur."* It was conceived in 1964 around the time of your first exhibition at the age of forty-three with which it shares, and I'm quoting here, "a predilection for certain angles and images." This London exhibition was first presented in Paris in 1982 in January. The title could be misunderstood, but in Caroline Tisdall's catalog she makes the point that "it has not to be interpreted as a personal statement about the artist's demise, it has rather more to do with reflecting a feeling about the world." I know that from the conversation we had here tonight in London that your feelings about the world have led you to consider making a sculpture on a gigantic scale, and could be involving you in personal expression of positive and optimistic energy at documenta this summer, and will be entitled appropriately for this, the seventh documenta, "Seven Thousand Oaks." It will be a celebration of many things, including the life of Jean Giono the French writer who told the story of Elzeard Bouffier, the French shepherd who, like you, believed in the importance of planting oak trees.

First of all, now that I've said that, I would like you to tell me how you can see a link between the present exhibition and this next step that you will take, this major work involving the planting of seven thousand oak trees at the documenta in Kassel. You see it as a natural and inevitable step linking the world of the artist with that of the ecologist and naturalist. You will concentrate all your energy on this and I would like you just to comment on this and in some way relate to this as a sculpture, involving very powerfully, from my viewpoint the dimension of time.

JOSEPH BEUYS: It is right, and you see already, in this title, the words "last space" appears, in relation to time. This is not as a demise for my doings. It puts a kind of line under my so-called spatial doings in so-called environments. I want it principally to mark the finish of this kind of work. I wish to go more and more outside to be among the problems of nature and problems of human beings in their working places. This will be a regenerative activity; it will be a therapy for all of the problems we are standing before . . . That is my general aim. I proposed this to Rudi Fuchs when he invited me to participate in the documenta. I said that I would not like to go again inside the buildings to participate in the setting up of so-called artworks. I wished to go completely outside and to make a symbolic start for my enterprise of regenerating the life of humankind within the body of society and to prepare a positive future in this context.

I think the tree is an element of regeneration which in itself is a concept of time. The oak is especially so because it is a slowly growing tree with a kind of really solid heartwood. It has always been a form of sculpture, a symbol for this planet ever since the Druids, who are called after the oak. Druid means oak. They used their oaks to define their holy places. I can see such a use for the future as representing the really progressive character of the idea of understanding art when it is related to the life of humankind within the social body in the future. The tree planting enterprise provides a very simple but radical possibility for this when we start with the seven thousand oaks.

DEMARCO: Why seven thousand, Joseph?

BEUYS: I think that is a kind of proportion and dimension, firstly because the seven represents a very old rule for planting trees. You know that from already existing places and towns. In America there is a very big town called Seven Oaks, also in England at Sevenoaks. You see that seven as a number is organically, in a way, related to such an enterprise and it matches also the seventh documenta. I said that seven trees is a very small ornament. Seventy is not bringing us to the idea of what I call in German *Verwaldung.* It suggests making the world a big forest, making towns and environments, forest-like. Seventy would not signify the idea. Seven hundred again was still not enough. So I felt seven thousand was something I could do in the present time for which I could take the responsibility to fulfill as a first step. So seven thousand oaks will be a very strong visible result in three hundred years. So you can see the dimension of time.

DEMARCO: It is beyond your lifetime and beyond the dimension of the twentieth century . . .

BEUYS: Surely . . .

DEMARCO: . . . or even the contemporary art world and you will see this as a first step . . .

BEUYS: I see it as a first step because this enterprise will stay forever and I think I see coming the need for such enterprises: tree planting enterprises and tree planting organizations, and for this the Free International University is a very good body.

DEMARCO: You can see young people all over the world becoming an army of helpers.

BEUYS: Right.

DEMARCO: All over the world?

BEUYS: Surely.

DEMARCO: You can see oak planting on the hills of Scotland or Wales . . .

BEUYS: and Sicily and Corsica and Sardinia.

DEMARCO: You can see the hillsides around Belfast beginning to be covered.

BEUYS: Everywhere, everywhere in the world . . . also in Russia . . . there are too few trees . . . Let us not speak about the United States which is a completely destroyed country . . .

DEMARCO: It is a sadness isn't it in our time that it is the United States which is growing rockets, and nuclear weaponry, rather than trees. Now you will make this statement to counterbalance this, in the middle of Kassel. Can you describe this enterprise more precisely.

BEUYS: I will start in very difficult places in the center of the town. There the places are very difficult because there is already coatings of asphalt and stone slabs with infrastructures of electrical things and the German Post Office. In the center of the town the planting of trees is most necessary for the people that live there within an urban context. There the planting of the trees will also be most expensive. The whole thing I guess will cost about three million German DM . . .

DEMARCO: And who will provide this money? You will have to work with the city fathers.

BEUYS: Yes, but they will not give money . . . the city will cooperate in so far as they will support our activities with tools.

DEMARCO: and gardeners . . .

BEUYS: and vehicles sometimes, but principally I took the responsibility for all of the money problems. I will fulfill this thing and ask many different people for support. I have received already help for the start of this thing, so for this year I have enough money to buy the stones because every tree is marked with a basalt stone. It's a natural form which need not be worked on as a sculpture or by stone masons. The stone is similar to what you will find in the basalt columns of the Giant's Causeway, but more triangular in shape with five, six, or seven angles or irregular angled stones which come from the volcanos . . .

DEMARCO: Will they come from the volcanos around Kassel?

BEUYS: It is very organic because this nearest volcano to Kassel is only thirty kilometers from the center of the town. It is very natural to take the stone to the place where I will plant the trees.

DEMARCO: What will be the date of the first planting?

BEUYS: It is already done . . .

DEMARCO: It is already done . . .

BEUYS: I planted the first symbolic tree in the center of the Friedrichsplatz. This is on the axis of the main building for the Documenta exhibitions and on the right side of this tree there is one stone already deposited. When the last of the seven thousand stones will disappear from this place it will say that the last of the seven thousand oaks is planted. That will be maybe in three years . . .

DEMARCO: That will be for three years and so that will last until the next Documenta.

BEUYS: That's true . . .

DEMARCO: Can you tell me, Joseph, just before we finish, how this tree project will allow you to continue your work on a new and wider dimension . . . this is a new dimension . . . it is a new step for you.

BEUYS: It is a new step in this working with trees. It is not a real new dimension in the whole concept of the metamorphosis of everything on this earth and of the metamorphosis of the understanding of art. It is about the metamorphosis of the social body in itself to bring it to a new social order for the future in comparison with the existing private capitalistic system and state centralized communistic system. It has a lot to do with a new quality of time. There is another dimension of time involved, so it has a lot to do with the new understanding of the human being in itself.

It has to make clear a reasonable, practical anthropology. It is also a spiritual necessity which we have to view in relation to this permanent performance. This will enable it to reach to the heart of the existing systems—especially to the heart of economics— since the wider understanding of art is related to everybody's creative ability. It makes it very clear and understandable to everybody that the capital of the world is not the money as we understand it, but the capital is the human ability for creativity, freedom and self-determination in all their working places . . . This idea would lead to a neutralization of the capital and would mean that money is no longer a commodity in the economy. Money is a bill for law, for rights and duties you know . . . it will be as real and will lead to a democratic bank system . . .

DEMARCO: It will, in fact, bring employment . . .

BEUYS: In fact it will organically prohibit every kind of unemployment, and organically it will stop inflation and deflation. This is because it deals with the rules of organic money-flow. This makes clear that all these interpretations of the future, especially the interpretations of time, have a lot to do with a new understanding of the human being as a spiritual being. If you have the spirit in focus, you have also another concept of time . . . you see time on earth is a physical reality. It takes place in space so it is the space/time relation which Einstein is speaking about. This already gives a kind of allusion to another dimension, but I think this other dimension is something we have still to detect . . . When I say we have still to detect it, it has already been detected. It is there as one dimension in my work which I show in the Anthony d'Offay Gallery. This is the warmth quality . . .

DEMARCO: The quality of warmth.

BEUYS: The quality of warmth. This dimension is, in fact, another dimension that has nothing to do with the space and time relation. It is another dimension which comes to exist in a place and which goes away again. This is a very interesting aspect of physics, since until now most physicists are not prepared to deal with the theory of warmth. Thermodynamics was always very complicated stuff.

Love is the most creative and matter-transforming power. You see in this context it is very simply expressed. Now it is not shown in very interesting diagrams which one could also bring to this discussion . . . But to promote this interest for all these necessities to the real anthropology and not this fashionable way of speaking about anthropology . . . in this relationship I start with the most simple looking activity, but it is a most powerful activity; it is planting trees.

Discussions of a few objects and
an action piece with Caroline Tisdall
1974 and 1978

RUBBERIZED BOX

(Gummierte Kiste) 1957
Ströher Collection, Hessisches Landesmuseum, Darmstadt

The outward appearance of every object I make is the equivalent of some aspect of inner human life. This box came out of my period of crisis in Düsseldorf-Heerdt and expresses my inner condition. My feelings then had this special kind of darkness— almost black like this mixture of rubber and tar. It is certainly an equivalent of the pathological state mentioned before, and expresses the need to create a space in the mind from which all disturbances were removed: an empty insulated space. Within this empty space investigations can take place, and from this concentration new experiences can emerge. This is a prerequisite for every experiment with the Theory of Sculpture: the principle of the insulator.

The nature of the materials used means this insulation has an elastic quality, softening the rigid form of the box which has nothing to do with minimalism. In addition it is significant that the box is open, which suggests that while everything else in the environment works as a distraction, energy directed towards or flowing from a higher level increases concentration. The mixture of asphalt and rubber on wood functions as a sound insulator, too. Asphalt insulates electric power, while rubber resists blows. With time its elasticity has gone and the surface has hardened, although originally you could knead it.

People will always bring their own association to such an object. Many think of the padded prison cell, for instance, although that was not my intention. While such a cell can be seen as a kind of insulator, such associations are too specific. On the other hand reference to extremes of isolation, as in the practice of prison control today, can certainly be sensed. The infliction of such isolation as punishment is an example of authoritarian pathology; but if an individual has the inner strength to survive it, it can, like pain, lead to new levels of awareness.

L A V E N D E R   F I L T E R

(*Lavendelfilter*) 1961

Collection, The Lone Star Foundation Inc., New York

Here the principle of the filter is related to the warmth process in plant growth. The lavender oil filtered through the cotton cone is a highly developed kind of fat produced by the flowers of the plant, and it evaporates up and out into the atmosphere.

The passage through a filter brings a refinement, a metaphor for finer quality which could be applied to the spiritual context. The filter at the base of the sculpture retains part of the oil as it spreads outwards in time and then becomes resin. The process of infiltration takes place as the filtered stain spreads slowly out-wards with time. This is the other side of the filter; a new refined essence, the spreading of ideas to the different force fields of human ability, a kind of inspiration that takes effect through a physical process of capillary absorption; psychological infiltra-tion, or even the infiltration of institutions.

Between the two processes of filtration and infiltration is the element of time implied in the object: the distance crossed by the drops, compounded by the duration of the spreading process. There is the smell, too, as ninety percent of the oil evaporates, leaving just a residue of resin. That is another difference between this highly developed etheric oil and the heavy fats like butter, which do not evaporate, though the smell of course permeates everything.

The association with wounds is often present in the filter, in the process of dripping, or the connotations of gauze as porous protection and absorbent bandage.

FAT CHAIR

(Stuhl mit Fett) 1963
Ströher Collection, Hessisches Landesmuseum, Darmstadt

My initial intention in using fat was to stimulate discussion. The flexibility of the material appealed to me particularly in its reactions to temperature changes. This flexibility is psychologically effective—people instinctively feel it relates to inner processes and feelings. The discussion I wanted was about the potential of sculpture and culture, what they mean, what language is about, what human production and creativity are about. So I took an extreme position in sculpture, and a material that was very basic to life and not associated with art. At this time, although I had not exhibited, the students and artists who saw this piece did have some curious reactions which confirmed my feelings about the effect of placing fat in a corner. People started to laugh, get angry, or try to destroy it.

The fat on the "Fat Chair" is not geometric, as in the "Fat Corners" but keeps something of its chaotic character. The ends of the wedges read like a cross section cut through the nature of fat. I placed it on a chair to emphasize this, since here the chair represents a kind of human anatomy, the area of digestive and excretive warmth processes, sexual organs and interesting chemical change, relating psychologically to will power. In German the joke is compounded as a pun since *Stuhl* (chair) is also the polite way of saying shit (stool), and that too is a used and mineralized material with chaotic character, reflected in the texture of the cross section of fat.

The presence of the chair has nothing to do with Duchamp's "Readymades," or his combination of a stool (!) with a bicycle wheel, although they share initial impact as humorous objects.

Now, fifteen years later, I can say that without this "Fat Chair" and the "Fat Corners" as vehicles none of my activities would have had such an effect. It started an almost chemical process among people that would have been impossible if I had only spoken theoretically.

SPADE WITH TWO HANDLES

(Spaten mit 2 Stielen) 1965
Ströher Collection, Hessisches Landesmuseum, Darmstadt

First of all these two handles on one spade signify a special kind of compound action for people working the earth together. Without the spirit of cooperation, harmony and even humor it would be impossible to work with the tool. Brotherhood and love are suggested by the heart shape of the iron blade, while the handles are like aorta or arteries. So there is a relationship to the bloodstream here, and iron too is an important component of blood.

During the action "24 hours . . . and in us . . . under us . . . landunder . . ." I held the spade at heart level and sometimes raised it above my head, which required balance. From time to time, the spades were rammed into the floor or thrown like spears. That made a hard acoustic interruption of the tempo, as often happens in my actions.

The relationship to agriculture is evident, as are the warmth and love needed for a regeneration of the earth. Spectators and visitors used the spades to dig furrows before and after the action.

The acoustic element and the sculptural quality of sound have always been essential to me in art, and in terms of music maybe my background in piano and cello drew me to them. Then there was the use of sound as a sculptural material to enlarge the whole understanding of sculpture from the point of view of using materials. Therefore not only solid materials like metal, clay, stone, but also sound, noise, melody using language—all become the material of sculpture, and also acquire their form through thought, so thought too is taken as a sculptural means. That is an extreme position, the real transcendental position of PRO-DUCTION in general.

The original Fluxus concerts were organized by people whose interest was in sound rather than painting or sculpture. Hence the link with John Cage, La Monte Young, and even Stockhausen and those concerned with electronic music. But their attitude was a revolutionary one and went against the traditional idea of the concert. Works were often presented simultaneously or followed quickly one after another. Often nothing more than a piano, a ladder and a pail of water were provided. The rest was improvised.

There were as many different ideologies and interpretations of Fluxus as there were people, and the chance to work with people of different opinions was one of the most challenging aspects. Anything could be included, from the tearing up of a piece of paper to the formulation of ideas for the transformation of society.

My first concert (apart from Beethoven at school and Satie at the opening of my exhibition in Kleve in 1960) was at the Galerie Parnass in Wuppertal in 1963. Dressed like a regular pianist in dark grey flannel, black tie and no hat, I played the piano all over—not just the keys—with many pairs of old shoes until it disintegrated. My intention was neither destructive nor nihilistic. "Heal like with like"—*similia similibus curantur*—in the homeopathic sense. The main intention was to indicate a new beginning, an enlarged understanding of every traditional form of art, or simply a revolutionary act.

This was my first public Fluxus appearance. I participated in compositions by George Maciunas, Alison Knowles, Addi

Koepke and Dick Higgins and presented two of my own works. On the first night I performed a "Concert for Two Musicians." It lasted for perhaps twenty seconds. I dashed forward in the gap between two performances, wound up a clockwork toy, two drummers, on the piano, and let them play until the clockwork ran down. That was the end. The Fluxus people felt that this short action was my breakthrough, while the event of the second evening was perhaps too heavy, complicated and anthropological for them. Yet the "Siberian Symphony, section 1" contained the essence of all my future activities and was, I felt, a wider understanding of what Fluxus could be.

[The Fluxus artists] held a mirror up to people without indicating how to change things. This is not to belittle what they did achieve in the way of indicating connections in life and how art could develop.

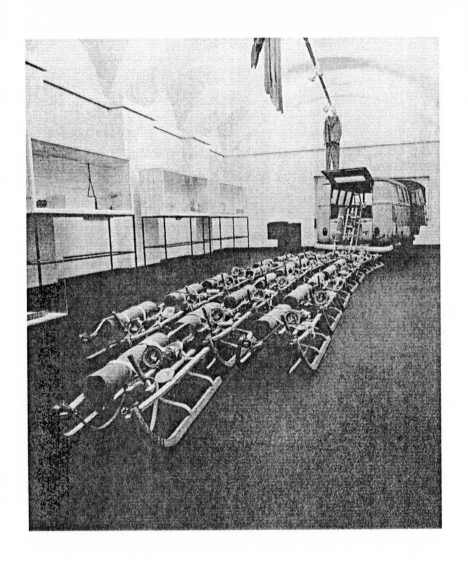

THE PACK

(Das Rudel) 1969
Collection Herbig, Kassel

This is an emergency object: an invasion by "The Pack." In a state of emergency the Volkswagen bus is of limited usefulness, and more direct and primitive means must be taken to ensure survival. The most direct kind of movement over the earth is the sliding of the iron runners of the sleds, shown at other times as a skating figure or suggested by the iron soles placed on my feet in "Eurasia." This relationship between feet and earth is made in many sculptures, which always run along the ground.

Each sled carries its own survival kit: the flashlight represents the sense of orientation, then felt for protection, and fat is food.

On a purely formal level, this, like "Vacuum←→Mass" is a filled sculpture, rare in art, common in life.

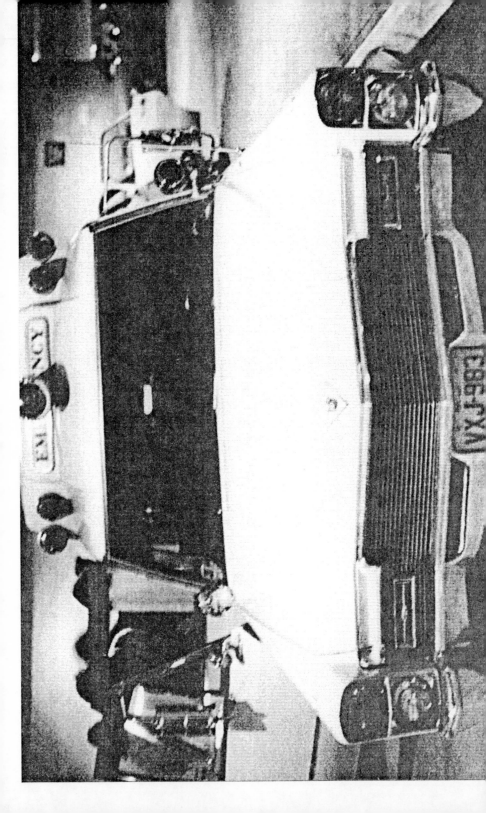

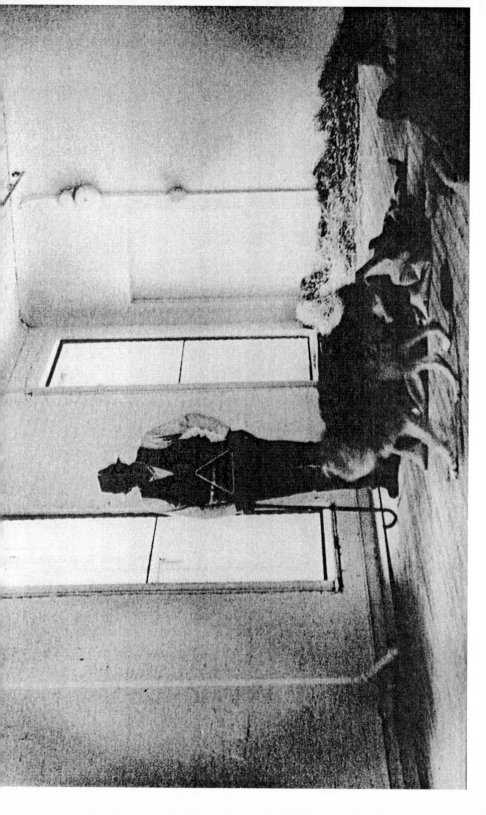

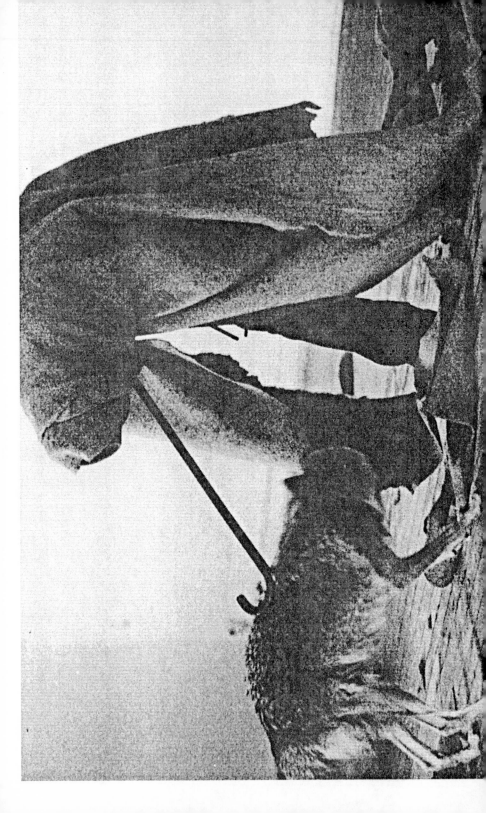

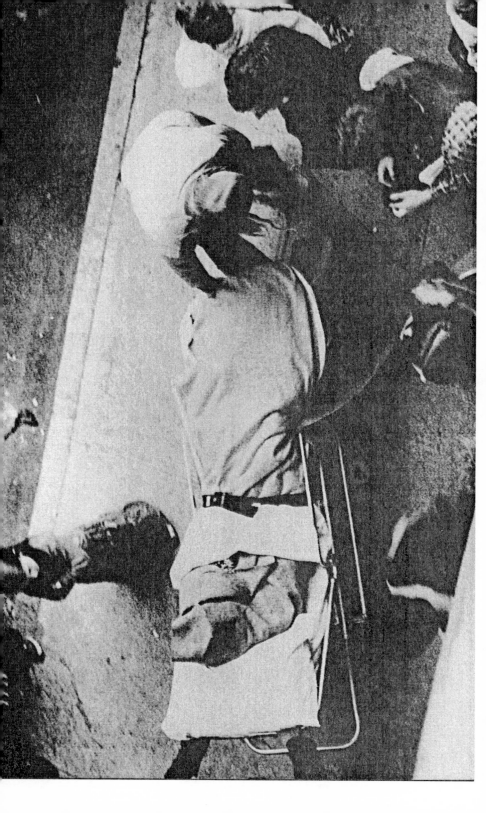

"COYOTE, I LIKE AMERICA AND AMERICA LIKES ME"

Action piece, 1974
René Block Gallery, New York City

I would never have done it with a coyote in Europe. But there are other animals in America which could conjure up a completely different aspect of that world. The eagle, for instance, the abstract powers of the head and the intellect, the West, powers that the Indian wore on his headdress. I believe I made contact with the psychological trauma point of the United States' energy constellation: the whole American trauma with the Indian, the Red Man. You could say that a reckoning has to be made with the coyote, and only then can this trauma be lifted.

The manner of the meeting was important. I wanted to concentrate only on the coyote. I wanted to isolate myself, insulate myself, see nothing of America other than the coyote. First of all there was the felt which I brought in. Then there was the coyote's straw. These elements were immediately exchanged between us: he lay in my area and I in his. He used the felt and I used the straw. That's what I expected. I had a concept of how a coyote might behave . . . it could have been different. But it worked well. It seems I had the right spiritual focus . . . I really made good contact with him.

My intention was firstly to hold together and retain in the West powers, and then to appear as a being representing the group soul area. I wanted to show the coyote a parallel power, but I also wished to remind him that it was now a human being who was speaking with him, and that's why my behavior was varied:

sometimes the image was more like a hieratic figure—a shepherd, but then, when I sprang out of the felt, I was quite an
ordinary man. And then the drooping tulip hat which had quite
lost its form made it just like the circus. What I tried to do was to
set up a really oscillating rhythm. First of all to remind the
coyote of what you could call the geniality of his particular
species, and then to demonstrate that he too has possibilities in
the direction of freedom, and that we need him as an important
cooperator in the production of freedom.

Why do I work with animals to express invisible powers?—You
can make these energies very clear if you enter another kingdom
that people have forgotten, and where vast powers survive as big
personalities. And when I try to speak with the spiritual existences of this totality of animals, the question arises of whether
one could not speak with these higher existences too, with these
deities and elemental spirits . . . The spirit of the coyote is so
mighty that the human being cannot understand what it is, or
what it can do for humankind in the future.

The triangle was intended as an impulse of consciousness
directed towards the coyote—it helped to restore his harmonized
movements. The confused roar of the turbine had to do with the
idea of undetermined energy. It could be seen as directly related
to the use of fat in my sculpture and actions—the point at which
fat appears in a chaotic condition. But the triangle has the
contained form of the front plane of the "Fat Corner" in my
sculpture: an equilateral triangle in which the undetermined
nature of the fat is completely integrated with determined, math-
ematical form. Since chaos or undetermined energy and crystal-
line form are polarities (extremes), the molding process in the
middle becomes the moment of transformation (movement).
According to the Theory of Sculpture, an action is a sculpture

dissected out into its essential elements. The turbine roar was also the echo of dominating technology: unapplied energy. This is energy that shouts down all discussion of energy in the wider sense, and in doing so has a chaotic and destructive effect.

The flashlight was an image of energy. First there was the storing of this accumulated energy, and then its gradual fading away during the course of the day until the batteries had to be changed. And here a curious crosscurrent developed. The coyote's energy pattern ran in a different direction: he was more lively towards the evening when the torch and daylight were fading, the light growing weaker and the shadows longer.

I did not want to show it as a technical device. It was a source of light, a hearth or heart, the glowing of a sinking sun or the gleaming of star energy in that grey hill.

The brown gloves represent my hands, and the freedom of movement that human beings possess with their hands. They have the freedom to do the widest range of things, to utilize any number of tools and instruments. They can wield a hammer or cut with a knife. They can write or mold forms. Hands are universal, and this is the significance of the human hand. They need not be specialized, and the diverse potential of their application stems from the fact that they are embryonic. They are not restricted to one specific use like the talons of an eagle or the mole's diggers. So the throwing of the gloves to Little John meant giving him my hands to play with.

Human universality—a total contrast to the *Wall Street Journal*: That's the ultimate *rigor mortis* afflicting thinking about CAPITAL (in the sense of the tyranny exerted by money and power) embodied unequivocally in a financial newspaper. A symptom of our time. That too is an aspect of the United States. But it is more than that—it is the diminished and destructive interpretation of money and economics, an inorganic fixation based solely on the production of physical goods.

That was the end of the sequence. But because it was a cyclic thing, you could say it was both the end and the beginning. That is the open situation out of which the next cycle flows. Everything is laid open again, and the new cycle is introduced. These were the instruments for Coyote, and that was the cycle. If I did it here with a bear they would be quite different. I could do it— here—with a bear . . .

F O N D   I I I / 3, 1979
B R A Z I L I A N   F O N D,   1979 (Background)
Dia Art Foundation, New York City

Any deposit of material awaiting the process of transformation becomes organic machinery. The generation of energy means the production of warmth, and hence the link with the idea of Social Sculpture and with the "Warm Time Machine"—another organic machine.

In "Fond II" the concentration is on the electrical charging of an object, in this case two tables thickly coated with copper. The tables have the connotation of a normal working place and become a "Fond" on which other objects can be placed. Through the process of induction and charging via the battery and the inductor a charge is released. It was exhibited several times in a charged state of 20,000 volts at documenta 4, at Eindhoven, and at Mönchengladbach. The charge from the 12-volt battery is transformed to 20,000 volts in the inductor so it is a high tension system creating big sparks, though the ampères diminish. In the object every stage of transformation is visible, though the sparks are scarcely perceptible in daylight.

The speed is important, and varies in the "Fonds." The charge is quick in this "Fond II" and in "Fond 0" with the copper lightning conductor, while the later piles of felt in "Fonds III" and "IV/4" represent a slow process of fermentation, induced by piling. So in "Fond II" the emphasis is on copper as a swift conductor, in contrast to the felt which acts as an insulator.

Principally "Fond IV/4" shares the battery character of other "Fonds." Nine piles of felt are covered with a top layer of iron, males rather than female. Iron and copper meet like Mars and Venus in the pile at the battery head of the "Fond" so the felt is completely enclosed with rigid materials. Unlike "Fond III" the arrangement is rigid: it can only be placed in this position like a train moving in one direction, or like a wall. Above it hangs the silent loudspeaker which does absorb but which transmits nothing.

Manifesto on the foundation of a "Free International School for Creativity and Interdisciplinary Research" 1973

JOSEPH BEUYS
AND HEINRICH BÖLL

Creativity is not limited to people practicing one of the traditional forms of art, and even in the case of artists creativity is not confined to the exercise of their art. Each one of us has a creative potential which is hidden by competitiveness and success-agression. To recognize, explore and develop this potential is the task of the school.

Creation—whether it be a painting, sculpture, symphony or novel—involves not merely talent, intuition, powers of imagination and application, but also the ability to shape material that could be expanded to other socially relevant spheres.

Conversely, when we consider the ability to organize material that is expected of a worker, a housewife, a farmer, doctor, philosopher, judge or works manager, we find that their work by no means exhausts the full range of their creative abilities.

Whereas the specialist's insulated point of view places the arts and other kinds of work in sharp opposition, it is in fact crucial

149

that the structural, formal and thematic problems of the various work processes should be constantly compared with one another.

The school does not discount the specialist, nor does it adopt an anti-technological stance. It does however reject the idea of experts and technicians being the sole arbiters in their respective fields. In a spirit of democratic creativity, without regressing to merely mechanical defensive or aggressive clichés, we shall discover the inherent reason in things.

In a new definition of creativity the terms professional and dilettante are surpassed, and the fallacy of the unworldly artist and the art-alienated non-artist is abandoned.

The founders of the school look for creative stimulation from foreigners working here. This is not to say that it is a prerequisite that we learn from them or that they learn from us. Their cultural traditions and way of life call forth an exchange of creativity that must go beyond preoccupation with varying art forms to a comparison of the structures, formulations and verbal expressions of the material pillars of social life: law, economics, science, religion, and then move on to the investigation or exploration of the "creativity of the democratic."

The creativity of the democratic is increasingly discouraged by the progress of bureaucracy, coupled with the aggressive proliferation of an international mass culture. Political creativity is being reduced to the mere delegation of decision and power. The imposition of an international cultural and economic dictatorship by the constantly expanding combines leads to a loss of articulation, learning and the quality of verbal expression.

In the consumer society, creativity, imagination and intelligence, not articulated, their expression prevented, become defective, harmful and damaging—in contrast to a democratic society—and find outlets in corrupted criminal creativity.

Criminality can arise from boredom, from inarticulated creativity. To be reduced to consumer values, to see democratic potential reduced to the occasional election, this can also be regarded as a rejection or a dismissal of democratic creativity.

Environmental pollution advances parallel with a pollution of the world within us. Hope is denounced as utopian or as illusionary, and discarded hope breeds violence. In the school we shall research into the numerous forms of violence, which are by no means confined to those of weapons or physical force.

As a forum for the confrontation of political or social opponents the school can set up a permanent seminar on social behavior and its articulate expression.

The founders of the school proceed from the knowledge that since 1945, along with the brutality of the reconstruction period, the gross privileges afforded by monetary reforms, the crude accumulation of possessions and an upbringing resulting in an expense account mentality, many insights and initiatives have been prematurely shattered. The realistic attitude of those who do survive, the idea that living might be the purpose of existence, has been denounced as a romantic fallacy. The Nazis' blood and soil doctrine, which ravaged the land and spilled the blood, has disturbed our relation to tradition and environment. Now, however, it is no longer regarded as romantic but exceedingly realistic to fight for every tree, every plot of undeveloped land, every stream as yet unpoisoned, every old town center, and against every thoughtless reconstruction scheme. And it is no longer considered romantic to speak of nature. In the permanent trade competition and performance rivalry of the two German political systems which have successfully exerted themselves for world recognition, the values of life have been lost. Since the school's concern is with the values of life we shall stress the consciousness of solidarity. The school is based on the principle of interaction, whereby no institutional distinction is drawn between the teachers and the taught. The school's activity will be accessible to the public, and it will conduct its work in the public eye. Its open and international character will be constantly reinforced by exhibitions and events in keeping with the concept of creativity.

"Non-artists" could initially be encouraged to discover or explore their creativity by artists attempting to communicate and to explain—in an undidactic manner—the elements and the coordination of their creativity. At the same time we would seek to find out why laws and disciplines in the arts invariably stand in creative opposition to established law and order.

It is not the aim of the school to develop political and cultural directions, or to form styles, or to provide industrial and commercial prototypes. Its chief goal is the encouragement, discovery and furtherance of democratic potential, and the expression of this. In a world increasingly manipulated by publicity, political propaganda, the culture business and the press, it is not to the named—but the nameless—that it will offer a forum.

CURRICULUM

1 Drawing	2 Drawing
Painting	Sculpture
Theory of Color	Plastic Art

Intermediary disciplines

Workshop	Joinery
Graphic Techniques	Metalwork
	Electronics
3 Theory of Knowledge	4 Social behavior
	Solidarity
	Criticism of Critical-behavior
5 Pedagogy	6 Phenomenology of History
Methodology	Phenomenology of Art
Didactics	Manifestation of History in Art
Critical Criticism	Criticism of Art
7 Verbal Articulation	8 Sensory Theory
Theory of Information	Pictorial Representation
9 The Stage	
Presentation	

INSTITUTES

Institute of Ecology

Institute for Evolutionary Science

All the terms contained in the syllabus are to be understood only in the context of the creativity-terminology as explained in the manifesto.

"Death keeps me awake"
interview with Achille Bonito Oliva
1986

ACHILLE BONITO OLIVA: Could you tell me something about the ideological intentions and meanings associated with the films *Der Tisch* and *Eurasienstab*?

JOSEPH BEUYS: If I could, so to speak, resort to verbalism or translate everything into concepts, I would have had no need to make films of this kind: I could have contented myself with merely writing down the concepts. This kind of filmmaking entails a whole range of things which don't readily lend themselves to interpretation. Consequently, in the case of *Eurasian Staff*, I would prefer to talk about what led me to make a film of this kind: i.e., a certain something which is European, partly Western and partly Eastern—in general. The tension between these two principles is well-known, even on a limited scale: if we draw a circle here in the center, we could say that, politically speaking, the tension manifests itself at the Berlin Wall: here we

155

have the East, and here the West. This has a bearing on the political situation, quite apart from the specific case of our country, Germany. It is a general European problem. One may ask how such a split in the East/West principle could have occurred historically. It is an event which dates back further than the last world war, a concept which has evolved through a long historical process.

BONITO OLIVA: Could you please explain why you chose these materials—the margarine, the felt covering on the beam, the iron sole? What was their significance for the realization of your idea?

BEUYS: As I said earlier, I would rather not go into questions of interpretation. I do not want to reveal the immediate meaning of the iron sole; I would prefer to talk about the idea which can be arrived at by a parallel route. Otherwise I would have to say once more what this or that means; in other words, I would have to provide a synthesis of the concept.

The "Eurasian staff" in the film is a long copper rod. The material is like an electrical conductor, i.e., it is a material through which something moves. To me, copper almost always has the properties of a conductor, and this conductor has a special shape and movement: it reaches a certain point, describes a sharp curve and then turns back part of the way. I believe it is evident that the rod has to go in this direction. I am certain—and I saw this from the East/West contrast—that the rod indicates the path from East to West. The rod describes a sharp curve and then turns back towards the East, and this means that something very significant originates from this direction; then the rod turns in this direction, which means that a particular complication has arisen, a sort of knot, and then the rod turns back. In my opinion, this is the beginning of a historical process. All developments in history originate in the East; it is only later that something evolves in the West, something which represents a kind of knot and then turns back.

Now, in view of the situation, there is the possibility of returning to the original direction. I said yesterday that Marx brought an Eastern idea to the West: this means that, sooner or later, the movement will return to its starting point and come to an end. This is shown by the fact that here, at the top, we have the head, the most important thing. Here I have indicated a source of radiation which—even in the film—appears as an electric conductor, a light bulb which meets the rod. Remember that in the past, it was thought that light originated in the East: *ex oriente lux*. Today this is no longer so: I think there is a possibility that the direction of the development may change and that light will come from the West, provided that man develops in a state of full awareness, as I imagine he will. It might be that the process which is now under way will continue: i.e., the process whereby Mao, for example, takes something from the West and transplants it to the East.

In our conversation yesterday, I also explained that only a part of our Western concepts can be seen as positive; here, in the East, the need arises for the development of new ideas capable of liberating Eastern man. I have already mentioned that Marx's teachings alone are not enough; it is necessary to work out something else in order to liberate all those people who are aware. Here we have a principle which has been transplanted to the West and wants to return to the East. As a head we have a radiation point, a source of energy: something which, using traditional symbolic language, can be called simply "the sun." So this is the head; here we have the primary energy, like a diagram which—in the case of Europe and Asia—actually passes across

Asia, moves the entire landscape and then turns back. Then, during the action, something is created, a kind of support. These filtering elements represent a sort of house: four filtering angles are built, and here the action is performed. Something is assembled and disassembled; there is something magical about it. The elements are not fixed, but are—like I said—dismantled and put together again during the action. Hence we can see, from a variety of angles, the impossibility of offering an exact interpretation. I can't deny that, seen from a certain point of view, all these images have their particular place, but I can't say definitely that the whole is a Gothic cathedral. I might say that it is a tent which is pitched and then struck.

BONITO OLIVA: Why did you use the organ as musical accompaniment?

BEUYS: Henning Christiansen and I discussed this at great length. I wanted a sound that seemed to come straight from inside the head. I wanted to set up a movement inside the brain, a kind of work which seemed to come from the head, the mind, on the one hand, and on the other was related to the notion of the plain, of flatness and space, which is present in the concept of Eurasia. Now, however, I'm not sure that I remember all the developments which I worked out so long ago and which subsequently took this form.

BONITO OLIVA: Your films and actions invariably contain informalist elements: one also sees links with the happening, with the Dadaist treatment of the object. Would you say that these references—to the happening, Dada, or *art informel*—are pertinent, or are they of no interest to you?

BEUYS: I don't think that there is any relationship with Dadaism, nor do I believe that there is any direct relationship with the happening; in fact, I feel that the very people—largely Americans—who coined the concept of the happening realized from the outset that I had done something which was very different from their conception; they realized instinctively that I was working against the happening right from the outset and that I was doing something else entirely.

For instance, I never thought that it was sufficient to have people participating in a performance from the standpoint of an outsider, leading them towards an activism which, for them, was devoid of all content. I also believe that the activation of man requires far more energy than this. In fact, the entire creative process must be activated; man should not express his feelings through a particular activity, such as breaking something, uttering accusations or destroying things. I never anticipated this sort of thing leading to the liberation of mankind: on the contrary, I have never expected anything from superficial activism.

BONITO OLIVA: I agree with you on the difference between your actions and the happening, since in your actions there is always a problem of communication, rather than one of involvement. Hence the problem of Eros is always present as a possibility of physical contact with the community. This is, I think, also shown by the use which you make of your materials.

BEUYS: The concept of Eros is a multifaceted one, and it may be that its meaning in Italian is different from in German: I am in no position to judge that. But I understand what you mean, and I think you're right. Communication, in which I am very interested, in my case manifested itself with such intensity that the people who understood it reacted in different ways.

Yesterday, I explained briefly how the material during the action is initially raw, chaotic and entirely shapeless; sometimes it is treated with heat to the point where it melts. I spoke about the heat generated in the course of this process, but I don't mean physical heat. I mean what you call Eros. By thermoplastic, I don't mean that it can be used to heat an oven; what I mean is a metaphorical concept of heat. As I said just now, this may be consonant with the concept of Eros. On the other hand, I am by no means satisfied with Freud, or let us say that I don't believe one can stop at Freud: one has to go beyond him. With Freud we are faced with a historical phenomenon similar to that seen in the case of Marx. There is no mention of some of the most important categories which—in my opinion—still require study. To this extent my actions can even be seen as a criticism with regard to Freud.

I am not saying that the body should be the most important means of communication, but that I have no other means of communication except the body. No other human being has any other possibility, because even when I talk, I use my body, i.e., my throat, my tongue and the rest of my body, to communicate. This is clear, but the body only has an indirect function; I have no interest in allowing it to act directly and thus transmit my body radiation to other human beings. On the contrary, what interests me is that my spiritual intention should achieve something; experience has shown me that each individual is reached in a different manner. It is necessary to show the intellectual that as a human being, he is in a position of extremism, and that, all things considered, he is sick. To this extent, the action is entirely therapeutic.

BONITO OLIVA: You speak of the passage from chaos to form. Your words remind me of Nietzsche, talking about the passage from the Dionysian to the Apollonian phase and the task of the

Superman in taming and shaping the wild forces of nature. Do you think that this is still valid under present-day circumstances?

BEUYS: I believe that it is still valid, to the extent that Nietzsche points out certain polarities, as in the polar opposition between the Dionysian and the Apollonian principles. The Apollonian principle clearly refers to form, the Dionysian to energy. The creative forces stemming from the subconscious find themselves in an extreme situation, as in the thermal process. Nietzsche sees the Dionysian as thermal, even magnetic in nature, while the Apollonian obviously has a character of form. Today, however, things of this kind must be seen as pathological images, in that they only show extremes. Although these extreme positions are useful in clarifying things, it must be understood that nobody is exclusively Apollonian or Dionysian: people are almost always a mixture of both. The concept of harmony could be introduced here. Harmony is extremely important today, although at one time the concept was discredited and considered bourgeois: this was because it had been wrongly used, with a false content. Today, concepts of this kind are taking on a decisive importance, with regard to illness and the manner in which it may be overcome. This concerns not only individual illnesses, but also— as we already said—personal illnesses.

If, for instance, I as a teacher meet someone, I know within a short space of time what to expect from this person. I could draw a person in this diagram and tell you what forces move him; in other words, if I am sure that he is solely determined by intellect, it is my duty to make it clear to him that he should acquaint himself with other forces. If he is here with a "strip of will," determined by blind activism, then I must draw his attention to the fact that he lacks form and that, in order to realize himself, he must think in this direction. This does not mean that he has to abandon his original position completely, but simply that he has to progress in his development, otherwise he would remain standing at the point determined at the time of his birth. I could remain as I am: either as a "strip of will" who smashes everything up, or as an intellectual, a positivist or an atomist who understands neither art nor man. However, the real educational process consists in people meeting each other and trying to understand their respective differences, learning tolerance towards others who are moved by entirely different forces.

We could draw what is necessary here. We could say that the head is here. It refers to thinking, i.e., to form, and usually thoughts are not located in the lower part of the body. When we speak of thinking, we are talking about the brain. Here I could draw a sort of figure, a shortened figure. The foot is here, and this is only a symbol: it symbolizes activism and the will. Here is the foot. This is precisely a man, standing, in the diagram and the action, at the angle of the margarine. We are talking about the brain, referring to interior movement, to feelings, to the circulation, and here to action, i.e., to the will.

BONITO OLIVA: I would like to know where you locate yourself in this diagram.

BEUYS: That, of course, is a good question, since I not only built these things but also experienced them. When I was young, I felt I was precisely here; hence the important place of the foot in my action. For a long time, I was dominated by will, until I realized that I was heading toward a crisis and would have destroyed myself if I had remained in that position. That is why I spoke yesterday about my attempt to reorganize myself. I was a veritable "strip of will," completely one-sided. I could also have become a boxer—that was my intention. You might ask me why I didn't stick with that. It isn't easy to explain, since other "actors" were involved as well as myself. If it had been left entirely up to me, I would probably have stayed where I was.

However, I believe that there are many things which help us in life, and I doubt that only human beings are involved. This is why my system does not only apply to the human question, but also to a form of organization which is superior to man. Yesterday I was asked why I am interested in animals. I answered that I am interested in animals because I am interested in a consciousness which is generally considered to be inferior to that of mankind. I want to make a dialectical use of it, since I am interested in the other aspect of the problem: you won't find me saying "Man is important, whereas animals are there to be eaten." I am also searching for the essence and the consciousness of animals and the possibility of a future development.

BONITO OLIVA: May I ask a silly question? At what point do you think you are today?

BEUYS: I'm not so foolish as to imagine that there is an easy answer to that. Someone should answer for me. Nevertheless, I believe that I have now acquired an extensive knowledge of these forces and their various effects. I have slowly attained an awareness. I can't definitely say that I'm here or there. You could say, however, that I have reached the knee: in other words, I have developed to some extent.

BONITO OLIVA: Why?

BEUYS: Because the knee has a particular significance at a later stage. Here we have the margarine. This is extremely important, and there would be a lot to discuss.

BONITO OLIVA: Tell me why.

BEUYS: In the first place because it is here that one starts developing upwards, but also for a number of other reasons. Turning back to the subject mentioned earlier, for instance, we know that the foot has a considerable importance for Western development. The foot is also a symbol of Christ. For this reason, the washing of feet later takes on a tremendous importance. Seen as a sign of the zodiac, the foot is Pisces. When we enter this zone, we are moving exactly in the zodiac, just as the times are moving now. There is the passage from Pisces to Aquarius, and the sign of Aquarius is located here, in the area of the knee, below the thigh. At present, we are leaving the Piscean age and entering the age of Aquarius. Here, the head, which is larger, represents consciousness. The wider the upper part, the narrower the lower section; the unconscious becomes conscious, in a manner similar to psychoanalysis. Psychoanalysis tries to render the unconscious conscious; the rest, the forces which make man chaotic and enslave him, can be controlled by the person himself and made conscious. In my opinion, this process is no different from the one which we follow to expand consciousness; insofar as this takes place, the unconscious is eliminated and becomes conscious. From this point of view, the need arises to make the entire history of mankind conscious.

We have to become aware of the method which history has followed. If we become aware of the methodology, we will be able to talk about the future, to develop a futurology. The concept of futurology is directly related to the concept of history. The concepts are reciprocally linked: in order to examine the future, it is necessary to have an awareness of the past. Needless to say, we must try and work out projects for the future, but we can only do so if we are aware of the methods of the past, of the methods of past revolutions, for example. At present it isn't quite clear that a partial analysis is being carried out of how the bourgeois revolution occurred and where it stopped. This means becoming aware of what is happening today. Marx did this in his own time, but he was alone and didn't get very far. What he achieved was a regression in the Soviet Union, where there really is no freedom.

BONITO OLIVA: Is your intellectual process similar to a social psychoanalysis?

BEUYS: Yes, of course. Art directly examines the psyche, the soul. Soul is not only soul per se: it also involves thought. It seems to me that the question of the nature of the subconscious is still under debate, from a new perspective.

BONITO OLIVA: You said that you disagreed with Freud.

BEUYS: The problem is difficult to discuss. I agree with Freud's diagnosis, according to which man lives to a considerable extent on his unconscious forces: however, in my opinion, Freud failed to work out a therapy or to state how such a therapy could be developed. The whole business remains confused. With Jung, on the other hand, things are rather more clearly defined: Jung finally showed that the unconscious has to do with history. Jung was the first to explain this concept, whereas Freud anchored it in sexuality, in a one-sided way. With Jung, the discussion is already centered on history. Today we should talk about the change in methodology, i.e., of how human nature has changed in the course of history, and how today a sort of anti-nature has evolved which is, so to speak, an enemy in the face of nature itself. To my mind, this context is extremely important. I didn't say I was an enemy of Freud, what I said was that something in Freud leaves me dissatisfied because it fails to provide a therapy.

We can now introduce a concept which is highly topical: the concept of the collective unconscious. Man is largely influenced by factors stemming from the past, i.e., by the collective unconscious. I would say that freedom is something dynamic which still needs to be developed. Hence man hardly ever knows how to use his freedom. We could tell man that he has the power to determine his own life, to change the repressive systems, but in respect of freedom, man is at a loss and doesn't know what to do. He must be shown gradually how to make use of his freedom; he must understand that he is allowed to do this. People who are active in politics are faced with a particularly tough problem when they acknowledge that man doesn't know how to use his own freedom.

BONITO OLIVA: Why is this so?

BEUYS: Man is considerably influenced by the past, by the forces of tradition; he has a number of reactionary aspects, because these forces are so strong that he has never "lived" his freedom and independence. If freedom has never been lived, it may be thrown to man *per verbum*, but he will not know what to do with it. It is only possible to do something if freedom has been lived and felt. This, of course, is the process of consciousness.

BONITO OLIVA: It seems to me that on the one hand you accept a certain part of what Nietzsche says, and on the other you correct what you don't like in Nietzsche by introducing ideas taken from Schiller: ideas about the liberating power of art, about its social function and educative role.

BEUYS: That's right. Schiller is a point of reference. He too talks about creativity, and he understood numerous aspects of it: he considers man himself according to how he appears in art. He could have taken this to its logical conclusion and said that man too is a work of art. He could have considered man as equal to art, equal to creativity.

BONITO OLIVA: I think that when you refer to Nietzsche saying that even Marxism had one or two correct perceptions to offer about the economic structure of society, you run the risk of indulging in a kind of shadowboxing, like someone who yet again opposes the individual to the collective structures of society: an individual who is a hero as long as he is himself and acts entirely alone, and whose image reflects his own aims rather than those of others.

BEUYS: The term hero, as it is commonly understood, does not apply to me, but to others. What is he to do? If he doesn't behave a little bit like a hero, if he doesn't use his strength, he won't change anything. However, I'm not talking about the kind of heroism which only acts in a particular situation: I simply mean the heroism which is necessary for a process of consciousness which requires all one's powers and demands that man should act effectively. I would suggest that this concept of heroism should be replaced by the concept of activity. The moment I cease to consider this concept of activity separately—so that instead of an external activity, it comes to mean an internal activity, a force coming from man—I reject the influence of the forces from the past, as they might perhaps be seen in a superficial understanding of Marx. Today, man actually has this possibility, the possibility of changing his entire nature, his own spirit. Here it is necessary to draw a distinction. I wanted to say that the concept of heroism should be replaced by the concept of activity.

The old concept of the family, which is now breaking down, is a true collective unit. Everything is in harmony, as it should be. People still say: "No, you mustn't do that. It isn't right." In a collective unit, everything is "right," everything is natural and requires no justification. There were customs and traditions which had to be followed: man had no real possibility of freedom; consequently we can say that freedom is something quite recent. To the extent that freedom is something new, the collective unit is overcome and becomes a subject of free discussion among people. In other words, if a joint work is successful, it can no longer be called collective: instead, it is a cooperation. I object to the fact that certain communes call themselves collectives. The term commune has a specific meaning, and to call communes collectives is atavistic and regressive: it means returning to a force which does not include the concept of freedom. In collective units, no mention is made of freedom. But the individual is vitally important.

BONITO OLIVA: When you talk about cooperation it sounds like "peaceful coexistence."

BEUYS: No, I don't mean that. Peaceful coexistence accepts everything that one's opponents bring out and tries to solve it politically. Peaceful coexistence means that I want to repress difficulties. A political system is worked out, planned in such a way as to prevent problems from rising to the surface. Hence I consider peaceful coexistence to be the biggest lie ever told. Coexistence doesn't exist, only cooperation exists. These are the exact concepts, the concepts of the past, which must emerge again: democracy, socialism, the concept of socialism as a Christian concept, love thy neighbor. This concept has to be developed further, and that is something which only the individual can do. All in all, socialism means love.

BONITO OLIVA: You have said that the silence of Marcel Duchamp is overrated. Could you say something about the relationship between your work and that of Duchamp?

BEUYS: In discussing his work it is necessary to avoid overrating his silence. I hold him in very high esteem, but I have to reject his silence. Duchamp was simply finished. He had run out of ideas; he was unable to come up with anything important. As I said, I have a great respect for Duchamp as an individual, but not for his silence, or at least I don't consider it as important as other people do.

All our discussions are excluded by the idea of silence. So far we have said that Marcel Duchamp's silence is overestimated. I would say that even the bourgeois tendencies in Duchamp's work—i.e., a form of provocative, bohemian behavior intended to *épater le bourgeois*—follow the same path. Duchamp started out from here and wanted to shock the bourgeoisie, and because of this he destroyed his creative powers, which really did atrophy. Here, as far as I am concerned, the silence of Marcel Duchamp starts to become a tremendous problem. Moreover, everyone knows that Duchamp was in the habit of reproaching young people by saying, "We have already done this, we have already done everything: actions, happenings . . . it's all old." How come everybody is so interested in Marcel Duchamp? Why hasn't anybody spent a bit longer thinking about Schiller or Nietzsche?

The content of Duchamp's silence refers to the aim of leaving the subconscious passive, of developing it. This is the aspect of Duchamp which is related to surrealism. The surrealists asserted that they could live with their subconscious; they thought they were way above reality, but instead they were beneath it. They thought that they could fish in muddy waters, fishing out lots of images, but to my mind, the images which emerged have a repressive effect. The fact that Duchamp was not interested in consciousness, in methodology, in serious historical discussion and analysis, makes me think that he was working in the opposite direction: i.e., he had reached a point where he was no longer working. He merely repressed his ideas. Duchamp's "silence" should be replaced by the concept of an "absolute absence of language."

BONITO OLIVA: What about the time before the "silence"?

BEUYS: Before that he had a language. He questioned a particular work. He should have joined in that discussion instead of withdrawing and thinking that he had made his contribution. Duchamp failed to solve or achieve anything. Had he come out into the open and discussed things, especially with young people, his work would have been productive, it would really have led somewhere, to concepts which would have been useful today. But—politically and aesthetically—Duchamp got nowhere. He refused to participate. Why? It seems to me that we must return to the concept of "absence of language." How could it be that he had nothing left to say? That he was without language, i.e., unable to communicate? That is the question.

   I only want to present him as a figure with a general significance, standing for a lot of other things. Looked at in this way, he offers useful negative information. But of course Marcel Duchamp is free to remain silent. I respect that. I hope that is clear.

BONITO OLIVA: In your opinion, did he carry out the first phase of this process of communication correctly?

BEUYS: Yes, inasmuch as he actually showed his work. His "*Pissoir*" was a genuine revelation, a work which at that time undoubtedly had a considerable importance, and he could have used it as a subject for discussion during the period of his silence. Several people have told me, although I'm not sure whether it's true, that Duchamp once said: "Somebody in Germany has been talking about my silence, saying that it is overrated. What does that mean?" I am convinced that he knew very well what it meant. If he was unsure about it, he could have written me a letter and asked me what I meant. Why not?

BONITO OLIVA: When did he say that?

BEUYS: In 1964. He could have written: "I read that my silence is overrated. Could you explain what this means?" That would have been better.

For some time now I have been working on a new idea: that Ingmar Bergman's *The Silence* is not overrated. I have a copy of the entire film. I had it mailed to me. I don't know if I should have done that. The silence of Ingmar Bergman is not overrated.

BONITO OLIVA: Perhaps one could look at it this way: that Duchamp recognized that a work of art only exists as such during the process of its creation, before it passes into the hands of a bourgeois purchaser.

BEUYS: Why? If a painting by Rembrandt is hung on a wall, does it make any difference whether it is a museum wall or a wall in a bourgeois house? Even if it is hidden away in a cellar, it doesn't lose its value as a work of art: its absolute function is preserved. It is not only a work of art, or let us say a work produced by the creativity of Rembrandt; it is a substance which is transmitted through time and doesn't have to be seen and admired by everybody. Something of this kind has also changed the development of human consciousness. A work of art doesn't necessarily have to be hung on a wall. I really don't understand why a work of art should be less beautiful in the house of a bourgeois than in a museum. It may be that the bourgeois is less careful than the museum curator, who is always on the lookout to see that nobody touches the work, but why should the work itself decline in quality or value? It certainly can't decay. Try though I might to imagine, from a material point of view, how it might decay, I just can't imagine it happening. The work remains on the wall until the moths get at it. Even then, though, there are still photographs or documents left.

BONITO OLIVA: Evidently when we speak of bourgeois art, we are not talking about the work of art itself, but about the fact that the function of art in bourgeois society is different from what it would be in a classless society.

BEUYS: So the bourgeois adapts the work of art to suit his own interests? That's true. Of course he tries to do that, but this has nothing to do with art, as a timeless idea. Today the bourgeois can no longer change the function of the works of Raphael or Leonardo da Vinci: the times have changed completely. Maybe the bourgeoisie can change the function of my art or that of Marcel Duchamp, but it will only be able to do so for a certain period, only as long as the era lasts, i.e., the era of the bourgeoisie with its particular method. But it should be clear that Marcel Duchamp, myself, you and everybody sitting here—all of us are still living in a phase of bourgeois revolution, since no other revolution has yet taken place. Even the Russian Revolution has reverted to a bourgeois revolution. All in all, the present time is still the outcome of the bourgeois revolution. This is perfectly clear, the way in which the middle class revolted against the old system by means of a revolutionary model. This model was really a scientific concept, and the revolutionaries were scientists—the Faradays, Darwins etc.—all those people who worked to prove that human beings can take charge of their own lives. Many more people were involved in the productive process during the bourgeois revolution, but after a time, the middle class isolated itself from the majority of the working class. The next phase will involve the whole of mankind in the process of education: originally, this was also the aim of the bourgeois revolution. Then the middle class discovered individual self-interest and went onto the defensive.

In order to defeat the bourgeoisie, it is necessary to develop a completely new concept of science. This is exactly what we are talking about: the limits of the concept of science which has now emerged and of an obsolete concept of art. We demand that both concepts should be extended. I have already extended the concept of art (however, I do not wish to claim exclusive credit for this; in this respect, even Marcel Duchamp achieved something). The concept of art has been extended. If I extend the concept of art to include the concept of creativity, I may also be able to modernize the concept of science and prevent it from remaining static.

The concept of anthropology must also be extended. There is a basic element in this concept: *anthropos*, man. It's very simple: man is in the center. Today, Lévi-Strauss and others have a different way of looking at anthropology. They turn their attention to the past, to myth, not in order to immerse themselves in mythology, but in order to examine it: in order to say, for instance, this is how man visualized the world as a whole at a given time. Our present-day concept of science is divided up into sectors and needs to be extended. In future, the concept of science must be redefined in holistic terms, in terms of materialism and polytheism.

BONITO OLIVA: Is there a concept of death in your work?

BEUYS: Yes, definitely. One may define death as the principle which produces specialization in materialism. A lot of people think this way and realize that this civilization of ours is dead, because of the excess of materialism and the narrow concept of science. However, if one looks at all this from a historical point of view, inquiring into the method of this concept of science and the reasons why it has become sterile, it becomes necessary to consider the entire history of philosophy, more or less from the time when myth and mythology underwent a change, when human nature was transformed by a methodology. Analytical thinking, which begins with Plato and Aristotle, leads to the emergence of the concept of natural science, of exact scientific thinking. That is the line of descent.

It may be said from a methodological point of view that the purpose of philosophy is to arrive at materialism, i.e., to move towards death. Ancient mythologies dealt mainly with life, whereas this line centers on death, that is to say on matter. Matter, of course, does not represent life: it consists of values which can be measured scientifically, but this act of measuring is centered on dead matter. This is the great mistake, since man is not a dead being but a live one. On the other hand, it is also clear that it is necessary to test death, that the phase of death must be passed through. Even with regard to future developments, death has to be conquered. In order to be able to say anything about life, one has to understand death first. In the first phase, one has to experiment with death: this subsequently enables one to think scientifically, in an exact, abstract fashion. This, I believe, is the methodology within philosophy: the methodology of reduction, the process of reduction. An alternative way of looking at this concept is to say that it has been proved (or that it will become apparent at some point in the future) that the first phase in the development of the natural sciences, i.e., the process of liberation, must necessarily pass through death.

Then a parallel process takes place. Here, the whole process is illustrated through which philosophy and science developed in the direction of materialism. This is the ultimate greatness. Now we can ascertain that Christianity manifested itself on the same plane as Plato. The question we then have to ask ourselves is: what was the task of Christianity? Actually, if we consider the phenomenon more carefully, we may observe that in the Church, Christianity has largely remained within its mythological framework. Whereas in my opinion, true Christianity developed in science. Philosophy, the concept of science, death, Emmanuel Kant, the process of abstraction: all these factors influenced the development of Christianity and enabled it to free mankind from the old collective unit. Methodologically speaking, it is obvious that man can free himself through the concept of science, but the first step is the process of abstraction, materialism. And this, it seems to me, is the path which the development of Christianity has in fact followed.

BONITO OLIVA: So Christianity evolves through abstraction, through Emmanuel Kant and materialism. A path which ultimately leads to death.

BEUYS: Yes. The true, simple Christianity—the Christianity of Christ himself, as one might say—developed in the West through the methodological progress of philosophy, of science, of extreme materialism, but it is a process of death. Examining it more closely, disregarding life and humanity, one realizes that its main feature has to do with the substance of death, seen in analytical terms. Christianity developed by realizing the concepts of science and materialism, and this is a headlong flight towards death, towards abstraction, and away from man.

In this case, however, man was able to develop himself as an individual: i.e., he succeeded in throwing off the ancient shackles. Hence with this method it has been possible to put Christ's promise of liberation and salvation into practice. Christ is the "steam engine."

We want to preserve the concept of death, but not in a one-sided form. It must be linked with the principle of life.

BONITO OLIVA: Where does your theory of angles fit into all this? What is your conception of the relationship between death and life, between the lower and upper regions? And what about nature?

BEUYS: I don't maintain that everything depends on death. If we were to discuss it now, the results would perhaps be too fragmentary. It would have to be tackled from a different direction. But we can ask if concepts, ideas, are all mental forms, if all this is represented by form. This is where things start getting serious. This is the most important thing: to find a theoretical basis for the next revolutionary step. To the extent that man is truly creative, i.e., to the extent that form comes from within as a form of free thought, we can even say that it is a sculpture or a work of art. To what extent is form truly free? Or is it conditioned by external factors? What is the relationship between the external world and what man does by and for himself? This is the really vital question, the point that decides everything, and also supplies the answer to the question about the next revolutionary step. So we have to carry on discussing this problem. Entertaining doubts is an excellent means of avoiding excessive credulity. And we no longer wish to engage in mere speculation: we want to have a real consciousness, a certainty and a consciousness. This is why the problem has to be posed in the form of a question, rather than making unfounded assertions. Continuing our train of thought, we arrive at the point where man brings something effectively new into the world: his form of thought.

I have to establish a limit, though: here we have a line—the environment, the surrounding world—and here in the middle is man. To what extent is man conditioned by the world about him? Can he himself contribute something to the world, something from the realm of ideas, which lies beyond the terrestrial, the material world? Can he contribute something new, something which is not of this world? Now we are faced with a theoretical question: what happens to the other actors? Are there any other areas? If we say: here is man, here is an animal, here is a plant, here is a rock, here is matter, and so on, then we are already talking about life, about feelings or instincts, and about consciousness.

To what extent can we say that no other consciousness exists here? Angles . . . I only want to speak from the theoretical point of view of consciousness. Angles, for me, are not mythological images. But I would rather leave this question aside for the time being and look at the extent to which it is possible to have other actors. Everything is decided at this limit. It is at this point that it is decided whether or not man is free. If he is conditioned by the environment, by what is already there, he can't be free; he can only be free if he is not governed by his environment. Of course man is always influenced by his environment, but if he is completely governed by it, then he is no longer free.

BONITO OLIVA: But he himself is a part of the environment.

BEUYS: Yes, but only in material terms, only in respect of his physical being. What I am concerned with is the part of myself which is not connected with the environment. This isn't just an academic point: the distinction I'm trying to make has a theoretical import. In reality things are somewhat different, otherwise our discussions would be endless. It is only from a theoretical point of view that one can decide whether freedom exists or not. If man is determined by his environment, then his destiny is to live in subjugation: he is not free. Any further discussion on freedom would be a waste of time; it would be purely ideological, bearing no relation to reality. When talking about freedom, one has to determine its foundations, and that can only be done by ascertaining its limits. We can say that freedom is possible, but freedom cannot come from the environment: it has to come from creativity.

BONITO OLIVA: What is your conception of God?

BEUYS: I shall talk about that now, but only theoretically. Firstly, I have to repeat an important concept. If man is determined by his environment, then there is no such thing as freedom. If freedom exists, it can only come from creativity. We said that freedom = creativity = man. Therefore freedom is achieved on the basis of the creative principle. And in that case, who else could be God, except man? If we don't want to go quite this far, we could say, using a scientific term, that God is a generator.

BONITO OLIVA: But if man is a god, how come he is faced with the problem of death? How does he deal with it?

BEUYS: Because he simply accepts death as a methodology of creation. Because he wants it for himself. Because he realizes deep down that without this element of death he would be unable to live in a properly aware manner. His life would be like that of a piece of seaweed. If he were only interested in life, he might just as well be a piece of seaweed. However, he is interested in death, i.e., in the spirit, in form. We can say that man is a god, or at any rate that he is an extension of God's finger, a cooperator.

BONITO OLIVA: A cooperator?

BEUYS: Yes. These are strictly theoretical ideas. I don't like talking about God, so I refer to the Great Generator, which is also a great machine, an electric generator.

BONITO OLIVA: Could you please enlarge on the idea of death as a methodology?

BEUYS: We have touched on a number of other concepts which explain, for example, that consciousness is impossible without death. Let's look at this idea more closely. I referred to certain concepts in order to show why death is the basis of consciousness. Because the entire development which takes place through Christianity, the development in philosophy and science, is a reduction of life. Our concept of materialism refers to a dead materialism, to chemical analysis, to statistics: these are all lifeless abstractions. Here it is clear that consciousness is impossible without death. It is only when I hit a sharp corner, so to speak, that I become aware. If I knock my head against a sharp edge, I wake up. In other words, death keeps me awake.

BONITO OLIVA: So in order to conquer death one has to look it straight in the eye and cultivate an awareness of it?

BEUYS: There is a contradiction here. It's very mysterious. I say that I wake up when death approaches, but "waking up" represents something living. Death is a means of developing consciousness, of achieving a higher life: a *higher* life, that is important.

BONITO OLIVA: As in Novalis, for whom night was the means of attaining knowledge, of finding reality.

BEUYS: Yes, definitely. All these things are only now emerging from obscurity. Novalis was born too early. He was pushed aside by a positivistic concept of science. But today, this is all very relevant. Now we can understand why it was that Novalis was born too early. We know why he went unheeded: because the line of death had not yet been reached. The line of death had to go right to the limit.

BONITO OLIVA: But today, death is closely associated with violence, isn't it?

BEUYS: Yes, it is: a fact which not only has to do with the failings of our political system, but also stems from this concept of science. The causes are only superficially political; the political forms are only the outcome of this development, which cannot be blamed solely on the bourgeoisie. One has to consider the whole historical development and look at the methodological steps involved; from this it becomes apparent that it is not just the bourgeoisie or the petit bourgeoisie which is the cause of our problem. The petit bourgeois period was a revolutionary phase; we are still living in it today. The cause is far deeper and has something to do with Christianity. This doesn't mean that Christianity is a failure, but simply that it was only a preliminary step, albeit an important one, and that Christianity—i.e., socialism— can only begin now, by thinking about death in positive terms.

THE SITE

III

Joseph Beuys and the Dalai Lama

INTERVIEW WITH
LOUWRIEN WIJERS
1981

JOSEPH BEUYS: Like the Pope, I think, the Dalai Lama should use his voice very far reaching, all over the world. I could with the Dalai Lama make a very important thing for television—worldwide satellite television—to participate in an information on the necessities of the time and on the philosophical content of such necessities. One must find an important formula for all these problems.

So, I think, the Dalai Lama could do a lot for this, he could promote a lot. He is a very important person in the world. He represents the spirituality of the East generally. Almost everybody has a slight idea of such a spirituality, and almost everybody sees at the same time that it is an old-time tradition, not able to fit the needs of the present time. But, I think, if an important correction could be made—if there is an interest in the general problems in the world—I think, then one could reach another level of importance for the Dalai Lama and for the development of such spirituality, having come from the past and going together with the present problems.

LOUWRIEN WIJERS: The Dalai Lama was, when he spoke to me, very interested in your way of thinking. He was very open to it. He said your way was the way to do it, to enter as an artist into the present problems.

BEUYS: I think it would be a fine opportunity to make such a very important performance or lecture or dialogue or interview. That would be very good. Then also there could be a permanent cooperation on the part of the Free International University—a very important practical enterprise, in which more and more people are getting involved. I think, there is a very practical thing to be done now. It is not enough only to speak, or to have private interviews. Now it should come to an organization, a very strong organization. The philosophies, they are very useful, of course, for such systems, and such proposals, and models, and formulas to solve the problems theoretically. But now they have to be solved practically by doing the things, by making a kind of network and organization.

WIJERS: Where do you think the Dalai Lama and you should meet?

BEUYS: That is now the next problem: where is a good place. (*Here Joseph Beuys remains quiet for a very long time.*) Where could be an important place in the moment . . . I must think . . . That is not so easy . . . [*quiet again, then*] Maybe the Documenta. Yes, very good. This time I will not participate in this official exposition style. You know Rudi Fuchs is doing it.

WIJERS: Yes, I know.

BEUYS: He asked me for my participation, and I rejected the plan to make a kind of sculpture there in this old way, to make in a kind of special place this special modern sculpture. I told him that my idea would be this time to plant seven thousand oaks in Kassel, seven thousand trees. And to mark every tree with a little stone, so that everybody after three, two, five or six hundred years can still see that in 1982 there was an activity. After the radical destruction of the forests here in Germany for all this technological nonsense, that there was an impulse that came in the same time, to plant seven thousand oaks. This is such a kind of activity during the Documenta, that has to do with the Documenta, but is a real other thing in the conventional understanding of art. So, we could there also have a meeting with the Dalai Lama. That would be, maybe during that time, a very good platform.

WIJERS: Very good.

BEUYS: I think this is a fantastic thing. There will be a possibility, and there we have also a very good output. Yes, sure . . . very good. It's a very good thing.

But I think one thing is necessary mostly, to do it not only once, to do it permanently. To have every three or four months another meeting so that the development of the events are always in the view. I think, that would be necessary to come to an international organization, like the Free International University, and to come to a cooperation and then to have a permanent connection. This is a necessity if one is interested in spreading out the ideas and in making a big effect and not only a kind of unimportant interview in which only a few people are interested. It has to appear like a light from a lighthouse that everybody can see. It is not only for once; it is a permanent junction, it is a permanent connection. It is a permanent kind of embracement of the East and the West—That would be a wonderful action and a wonderful thing—that is the optimum, the maximum of possibilities in this respect. And I would be interested to make things as good as possible.

WIJERS: How should I describe the Free International University in a short but clear way to His Holiness the Dalai Lama?

BEUYS: The Free International University is an institution to develop an alternative against the Western private capitalistic system and the Eastern central communistic ideology—so against the two most important economic concepts now ruling and destroying the world. That is the most simple description. We are developing the new structure for the spirit of freedom, equality and brotherhood, for solidarity in the economical field, for real democracy, for a real other structure of state and money problems, a new structure for enterprises. Then the Free International University wants not to work only theoretically . . . she wants also to develop her reality as an enterprise.

We have a small budget now, from givers, small allowances from different sides and also from my own work. So, we want to be an enterprise for ourselves, which produces insights, and which produces also physical goods. So, it is an economical enterprise integrated with a spiritual enterprise. I think, that is the new constellation for every enterprise in the future. Every working place, every industrial entity should be at the same time a universal unit to overcome the alienation of the people who are working there. So, this would lead to a whole social body with spirituality, and not only so-called culture, theater, and this conventional exhibition activity and modern art activity in museums only. That's not enough. Culture should exist on every working place and on the highest levels possible.

Then, I think, it is also important maybe to tell that the Free International University belongs to a social movement of which the Free International University was a co-founder, the Green Movement, an ecological movement, and that we participate in the ecological development of the different spheres: agriculture, pollution, education problems and so on. So, we are firstly an enterprise, a cultural institution, a research institution, then we are linked with the ecological movement, especially with the Green Movement.

And surely one can also tell that one part of this Green Movement has a parliamentary arm, that they try to reach and influence the parliaments, that they want to compete also in elections; and that they did already and are already sitting in some regional parliaments. Not in the federal parliament until now, but, I think, in two years when there is another federal election, then we will also be sitting in the federal parliament. And, I think, from such a place there could be a lot of influence produced. We are denying the other political parties, but we want to have influence within the existing parliaments to transform the parliamentary structure. Therefore we have developed this parliamentary arm, since we have to follow the legality of the system, the legality of the descriptions in the constitution. So, we have to be a political party, otherwise we can't participate.

If the Dalai Lama wants to have information about the whole system and how we work, then one can say: We started in 1967 with the Student Movement. That first period was called the Organization for Direct Democracy. In 1971, I transformed the organization into the Free International University, and two years ago I was a co-founder of the Green Movement, and later a co-founder of the political party the Greens. So, then one has a simple image of what is already organized in a way. We are also linked with the peace movement; so, we are therefore strictly against nuclear weapons, especially in Middle Europe between the two power blocks of Soviet Russia and the United States. It is our daily struggle to work against these destructive armament competitions. And also we want to have influence as early as possible in the Eastern Block countries, like how to behave now in Poland, and next week I have a meeting with seven or eight people from Russia. So, there are already a kind of underground connections, sometimes very small, not enough. But also in a meeting like we may have with the Dalai Lama we could reach a very modern information on spirituality. At least one can think about a fantastic network, which has its roots in Asia.

I think we have covered the general view on what we try to do, stressing the spirituality, stressing the absolute truth and the way to find this truth together also with other reasons, maybe with the Dalai Lama and his people, to come to an embracement of Asia and the West. And then we have to reach the economical structure, and the conviction that we cannot stay apart and make things happen only in so-called cultural corners. This will not have enough effect on the system. So, we have to develop a proposal for another kind of economy, and law, and a liberation of the cultural institutes. The idea of freedom is the central idea of all, and finding not only the world in a state of freedom, but bringing also the enterprises to the state of self-organization. And after having done this it would be very easy to fulfill the needs of the people all over the world—solve the third world problem economically. But to have influence on the monetarian element we have to start in the high developed centers. It should therefore start here. Now we can realize Eurasia . . . my old concept Eurasia.

WIJERS: Do you think that in a further stage Andy Warhol might want to cooperate?

BEUYS: I think so. I think he would be very interested in the moment when the Dalai Lama appears, being involved in such a kind of idea. Andy has always difficulties with this kind of political activities, because he works in another kind of world, but he is always . . . Also again when he was here last week, he is very interested to hear a lot of new information. He has a kind of observing sense in the back of his mind. So, he is always interested to follow the development, and there is really a kind of imaginative process going on, I think.

WIJERS: He thinks about things and then he gives a very simple answer.

BEUYS: Yes . . . yes . . . that's right . . . that's right.

WIJERS: But he is completely with it, for instance, on the level where you are working, only he simplifies it.

BEUYS: That's right.

WIJERS: Andy Warhol did already quite some years ago an interview with the Dalai Lama in his magazine *Interview*.

(Joseph Beuys looks at an article I had just finished and that I have brought for him. He reads the title: "Answers from Interview with the 14th Dalai Lama of Tibet Compared to Answers

to the Same Questions as Given by Joseph Beuys and Andy Warhol.")

BEUYS: A fantastic title . . . ha . . . ha . . . ha. A wonderful title . . . Dalai Lama, Joseph Beuys and Andy Warhol . . . a good trinity.

WIJERS: I thought so too. Three very important persons of our time.

BEUYS: Ha . . . ha . . . ha . . . ha . . . yes . . . a very, very fine constellation . . . very interesting.

CONVERSATION BETWEEN
LAMA SOGYAL RINPOCHÉ
AND JOSEPH BEUYS
1982

JOSEPH BEUYS: Louwrien Wijers has already had contact with His Holiness the Dalai Lama. She did already speak about the intentions which I and my friends try to develop in the Western world. My personal relationship to these plans is an interest in the Buddhist philosophy as a special personal fate. I could say that I am a friend of the tantric intention, and . . . I could say, from the point of view of my astral body, I was already in Tibet—not to speak about incarnation and reincarnation, which is also a necessity to bring to the people—in order to come to another understanding of the values of life and death and death and life . . . and again.

The Free International University is an organization that has a lot of offices in Germany, in the Netherlands, in England, Scotland, South Africa, Scandinavia and so on. I think, what we should do is not to make a little thing. It should be a big—a great idea.

LAMA SOGYAL: I agree with you.

BEUYS: . . . that has the kind of willpower that will bring some new spiritual intention on this planet firstly—not to speak about other planetarian states in the future, other later states of the planetarian unit. For that, the necessity is in my understanding, to prepare a kind of living body on this planet, which could transform towards futural existences. Maybe this is my first sentence.

LAMA SOGYAL: I am sure you know of His Holiness the Dalai Lama, what He represents and also, what He is trying to do. Apart from the fact of being the leader of the Tibetans, He feels very strongly that His duty is not only to the Tibetan people but to our humanity as a whole. And He has been speaking time and again on issues of a similar nature, where the emphasis is on how to use the good human quality, such as the Good Heart. He always speaks about that. And His message has always been on "universal responsibility." For He feels that maybe the West is slightly shortsighted in its vision, in its approach, and because of that, they always end up with many problems. They try to solve immediate problems, but in the long term they are creating more problems and are further intensifying them. His Holiness has a great following, but it is my personal feeling that the time is right for His Holiness to really express Himself in the world and work with people like yourself and others. And I hope that will happen.

BEUYS: That is what I hoped too. We in the West, we have also a kind of spiritual issue as a certain basic underground that is an ancient tradition, which runs through very old Christian impulses and through Rosicrucian intentions, and is being carried by people like Rudolf Steiner, for instance, in his so-called anthroposophy. These still functioning spiritual impulses in the West could make a bridge between the spirituality of the West and the spirituality of the East to find the connection with the cosmic spirituality. This again is the basis of every activity. I think, that we have a lot of sects, so-called spiritual sects, that tend to isolate themselves and to care for a kind of private spirituality, which is not open towards the problem. But what I have always felt is, that the tantric Buddhist form would maybe have the most possibilities to carry out this openness.

LAMA SOGYAL: I think so.

BEUYS: . . . being radically and clearly related to all these effects of humankind's work—what they do with their hands, what they feel with their soul, what they think with their consciousness. And, I think, it is almost a necessity that such old traditions appear with a very modern futurology so that the people can see that the Buddhist intention, the reality of the Buddhas and Bodhisattvas, is not a historical, symbolic museum; but that it works through life.

LAMA SOGYAL: That's true. For instance I have personally been feeling . . . I have now been working in the West for about ten years, and coming into contact, a little bit, with the Western mind, I find a kind of neurosis. People have a kind of chaos, but also a kind of understanding, a receptivity, the good and the bad. It is crazy, but yet also very sane.

BEUYS: Sure.

LAMA SOGYAL: I feel this is a very right field, in a sense, for tantra which, in a sense, is very much an art in itself. We always talk about tantra in terms of skillful means, which really, in reality, it is not. It is a spiritual art.

BEUYS: True.

LAMA SOGYAL: And, I think, there is some way of really connecting that approach with the expression of modern art or with art as it is happening now.'

BEUYS: I do not call this the period of modern art . . . since the so-called modern art is only a synonym for the attempt of the Western world's soul to get free and independent of every predetermination by the political pressure. But for me this is not enough . . . this modern art—it has to come to a wider understanding of art, which could be related to every person's doing. So, the formula is: "Everybody is an artist." Every human work has to be seen as a kind of art. For me only this idea could overcome this fragmentation that we have now. There is the world of art, there is the economics, there are the law problems or, the so-called democratic problems, there are the cultural problems, with the school systems, the university systems, the education. To see the world principally as a unity with the idea of creativity and ability of the people, it means their spiritual constellation with all their real creative powers, thought powers, soul powers, will-powers, etherical powers, and all the further and higher developed bodies. This is a necessity—to overcome this completely distorted and only additional nothingness. Nobody knows anymore what one is working for . . . where the goal is . . . how to develop and unfold the powers of the world.

So, I see that the values of the West try to split away from the spiritual grounds, in order to come to a very strong and systematic analysis of the material condition only. So, the man in the West is bound to material powers.

LAMA SOGYAL: I feel that with this particular age, beginning with the sixties or, I don't know exactly when . . . but, I feel that the real kind of human energy has been unleashed.

BEUYS: Yes.

LAMA SOGYAL: And what modern art has done is—it lets you see it is there, but you're just left there and you don't know: Now to do what?

BEUYS: That's right.

LAMA SOGYAL: . . . and that is where you have to take it, to mold it. It is very interesting, for instance in the tantric teachings, that with any particular expressions, or changes that happen as they hit you, at the moment of reaction, like a shock, or whatever to not watch the object of the art, at that moment of reaction, but to watch the mind . . . the artist, so to speak and then to understand the nature of the mind, and then to work with the artist in a sense—to work with oneself. And so, this is where, I think, really art could be carried on to.

BEUYS: Yes.

LAMA SOGYAL: Also for instance in meditation when you use the "out-breath," just the "out-breath," first you think: "I am breathing out." Slowly, slowly the "I" goes away: "Am breathing out." Slowly, slowly "am" dies: "Breathing out." So that one becomes functional. In function one is there. One is the action. One is happening—so pure, so fine, that one becomes almost a dot. And in that dot one begins to develop a certain poise . . . a poise, and a clarity vision out of which comes the art.

So, it is very interesting to mold this. And then, as the perception becomes clearer, how to then transmute neurosis with the perception that one has developed—through art for instance. The artist is great. He has a tremendous original mind, but the rest of the time he is also quite crazy . . . ha, ha, ha. So, what do you do with that expression that you get. How to use that?

BEUYS: Bring everything in the evolution of humankind and the world to another stage. That must be the goal.

So, the Western world is crazy! Some parts of the Eastern world . . .

LAMA SOGYAL: are crazy . . . ha . . . ha, ha, ha.

BEUYS: You know it . . . ha, ha . . . ha . . . ha. The value of the Western world is to have given a kind of strong analysis of material conditions—in physics, in chemistry, in medicine, on material principles. But this is only a very, very small sector of the whole truth of the powers of the world. Now we have to come to a completion and a new organic overcoming.

LAMA SOGYAL: So, how do you feel you would want to work. In what way do you think it can be begun?

BEUYS: It would be very fine to have in the very near future, if possible, a meeting with His Holiness the Dalai Lama to develop a feeling of brotherhood firstly and of a fate where the actors belong together as a kind of embracement. So, it is an act of love. If this would take place more often, and on especially very important points then this would give, I feel, an example for millions of people.

Maybe His Holiness would be interested to meet in Japan. There is a great interest in all the new intentions that the Free International University develops on the nature of humankind's labor, to come to a real other structure of the social order, and to come to the richness of the social order, while now the social order is indeed ill. So, there would be a possibility to meet in Japan. And, I think, there would also be a necessity to go to Beijing. I know that the Chinese people are looking for a real other concept of labor, of organizing the work, and are thinking on the nature of culture—how it is linked with humankind's laws and civil rights—and how our ability could be applied, that means our artistic ability, how that could work in what we call the economy . . . an economy that is an organic unity of the spirit with our physical labor. And vice versa, how our physical labor could work with our spiritual development, in education, and in a permanent developing of every creative power.

The idea of creativity is for me the problem of the future. Since the creative power is not a simple thing. It has a rich structure. It is divided into a lot of different principles and represented by figures, and these figures you can also write down in a kind of symbolic mantra. It is important to work on every point of creativity and see how the human being stands in the energy that comes out from the surrounding world.

LAMA SOGYAL: Particularly the younger generation. What do you feel of the really young generation?

BEUYS: Exactly, the young generation is craving, is yearning, is looking for such a kind of idea. They are empty now, and while being empty they are going the traditional way of making a kind of career and making a bit of money. But most of the people are yearning and craving for a content.

LAMA SOGYAL: I think, the point would be for Louwrien to again talk with His Holiness. And I also would be very happy, with my limited knowledge, to share with you whatever I can in this particular field to then slowly come to an understanding, for instance in the field of action. I think, a plan of action should be brought out; what is to be done in the field of education, and, how to meet with other people, other leaders and so forth. Because somehow, sometimes even when there is a tremendous affinity, when many, many people are thinking of the same thing the difficult thing is coming together. That is what we call "auspicious coincidence."

BEUYS: There is a necessity to have a permanent conference on the questions of humanity.

LAMA SOGYAL: Very important. I think, it would be a very positive and wonderful thing for the future, for mankind.

BEUYS: For me personally it would be interesting to learn how the tantric power is organized and working. The Tibetan tantrics are now rejected out of their own country Tibet, but, in my vision, there exists a possibility to come back also.

LAMA SOGYAL: Exactly. It is very clear that we were thrown out of Tibet; we didn't leave as missionaries, we were literally thrown out of the country . . . by history. I think, it could be that, though unfortunately Tibet had to suffer in this particular period of time; it is a kind of evolution. Because at that particular moment there was a whole new awakening beginning to happen in the West, with art, with music, and so forth. That, I think, is very, very interesting.

BEUYS: This historical event, you could say, as a collective karma now has to develop its value.

LAMA SOGYAL: Exactly.

BEUYS: That is the whole figure. I see it as a fantastic possibility.

LAMA SOGYAL: Very important. We had this very great master called Padmasambhava, who brought the teaching to Tibet, and one thing he said was: "In the future people will complain that times are bad." He said: "It is not the time. It is the people. It is the people who make time."

BEUYS: Yes, sure. That is just exactly what I always say: "The human being is the producer of the time."

LAMA SOGYAL: Time is only a sense, only a sense. So, I think, it's very important to—I am very direct.

BEUYS: That's fantastic.

LAMA SOGYAL: . . . and I will tell you that especially with this kind of work—it is such an important work—but sometimes also there are negative forces that are at work. So, therefore you must tread with double caution. That is very important.

BEUYS: In this moment where such a thing goes on a lot of enemies will appear, counterpowers will appear. But in a way we are already trained in getting ready with all the counterpowers. The necessity remains to be very cautious, even more cautious, in acting out such a plan. It means, doing it after having thought with the highest responsibility and after having a good agreement with all the participants around the table in this permanent conference. I think, this should at least give a very important impulse.

LAMA SOGYAL: The impulse is necessary, really necessary, because at the moment there is a tremendous yearning, as you say, and also an emptiness, which needs a kind of a lead. To spark that off—that is important.

I am sure you have much more experience, knowing how the time is happening. I travel quite a lot, all over teaching in my little ways, and I find that there is something happening with the young people. In a sense it is that they no longer have anything to follow. So, they are beginning to feel very rebellious sometimes. They are beginning to feel that life offers nothing.

BEUYS: Yes.

LAMA SOGYAL: So, this is a very dangerous thing. And somehow that energy could be transmuted and awakened.

BEUYS: That's right. So, then I'm thankful for this meeting.

LAMA SOGYAL: I'm happy to have had contact with you.

BEUYS: Then, I will not cover too much of your time.

LAMA SOGYAL: No, it's fine. I have just come back from Athens, half an hour ago.

BEUYS: That's wonderful. I'm very thankful. This was already an act of reality. Now there exists a connection.

LAMA SOGYAL: I'm sure, you know, something good will happen.

BEUYS: Are you often in Athens?

LAMA SOGYAL: No, actually my main work is in London and Paris. But also I go to the United States. I travelled twice to the United States.

BEUYS: You are mostly to be found in Paris or London?

LAMA SOGYAL: Yes, and then also I teach in Italy sometimes.

BEUYS: So, if I come to London, I can ask for you?

LAMA SOGYAL: Yes, please. I give you my address and please, be in touch. And I could be, may be, a small piece of the jigsaw puzzle.

BEUYS: That's very wonderful.

LAMA SOGYAL: And also I would be happy some time in the future, when we have time to also talk about art and things to learn from you. So we are sure to know each others approaches. That is very important. I know, one could read from books, but sometimes it is better to hear from persons directly.

BEUYS: Yes.

LAMA SOGYAL: . . . rather than read books.

BEUYS: Louwrien knows, that my actions during the last years have mostly been to speak with people—speaking with the people, and sometimes making a kind of diagram on the blackboard to make some formulae, some principles, some regulations very clear. To make clear that there is a kind of inner structure of the whole thing that there is a regulation, that there exists, what we call in the Western world, this so-called objectivity, that doesn't exist from another point of view.

LAMA SOGYAL: Exactly.

BEUYS: From another point of view this is all just to solve this paradoxical understanding of how the powers work together. How for instance, the light which has no color, comes to color and works together with magnetism, atomic structure, and all these things. There is an interchaining of all these things. But, so the people do understand that there are many different figures existing and that all are working together. So that the people don't work only one-sided, because this comes mostly to egoistic behavior. So, this is my way to speak and to make sometimes a kind of structure.

LAMA SOGYAL: It is, for instance, very interesting. In the highest teachings of Buddha, in tantra, it is called *Dzog Chen.* There it says that the transmission is in three ways: first is the mind-direct—no signs, no words. That is the kind of communication that the Buddhas have, the direct, mind-direct. In some ways it is not even telepathic, there is not even any time wasted. It is simultaneous . . . as it happens.

BEUYS: Unity itself.

LAMA SOGYAL: True, unity itself. And then, the next level is: how it was translated in terms of a human need, as a compassionate incarnation or whatever. By signs—signs that were may be just a syllable or a gesture. So that, through that it is transmitted to people who are able to tune into that are able to capture the meaning. Then, by word of mouth, the oral transmission. And oral transmission again is really, actually a mind-to-mind contact and then conversing on that basis.

So, it is very important, I think, to work with the signs, and art, it definitely is very much that. And art . . . my personal understanding is, that art draws a balance between pure mind and the expression.

BEUYS: That is really true.

LAMA SOGYAL: It is like almost pregnant.

BEUYS: Yes.

LAMA SOGYAL: It is a kind of having given birth, but the umbilical cord is not yet cut.

BEUYS: That's right.

LAMA SOGYAL: I think, there is a link between this and the tantric teachings. Very much so. . . .

BEUYS: In the Western world there is one result for all the needs, that is coming from this one-sidedness of working with the so-called analytical science—the positivistic, or atomical, understanding of the world—that was for many natures in the Western world the cutting of an umbilical cord. So then, the people were completely alone. This is also a kind of fate, a kind of karma.

How to develop from this position where the umbilical cord is cut away from the cosmic powers. Now the people have to come to their own recreation. That pushes the willpower towards a special point. Now we are standing before a big wall. With this potential power coming from being very lonely, left alone, in this analytical field now we have to break through the wall. That is, for instance, the theme in all this very important Western world's poetry, like Beckett. They are knocking on the wall, but they are still isolated. They are still sitting in the garbage can. And now they are knocking on the wall. This comes more and more as a voice not only to the outer ears, but to their inner hearing. And, I think, that is the fact of the Western world's karma and position. And this is also a problem of Christianity.

LAMA SOGYAL: I think, it is the theistic approach. I think, the whole problem arose with the concept of God. In very many ways God is fine. For instance, from a Buddhist point of view, we are not against God at all. In fact, that is fine. But it is the idea, the concept, which is another way of, we, enhancing our ego. For instance, when Moses and God met and God told Moses: "I am who I am."

BEUYS: Yes.

LAMA SOGYAL: Then we immediately . . . we do not understand it in terms of God's language saying: "I am who I am." But we understood it from our language: "Oh. I am who I am. Oh, I see." So, it becomes immediately a reference point for the ego . . . very much that. So because of that dualistic thing, it is very difficult. When you, for instance, bang the wall you end up at the wall.

BEUYS: Yes.

LAMA SOGYAL: The investigation of the mind, the Creator or whatever you might call it. That is important.

BEUYS: All these things are so much a very important theme to investigate or to meditate on. For instance, this meeting of God with Moses . . . or Moses with God in the Burning Bush. This being meditated upon would show that there is a real other understanding than the monotheistic concept.

LAMA SOGYAL: That is true . . . very true.

BEUYS: The monotheistic concept is the Jahveh principle and that is the karma of the Jewish history and of the Jewish people. They cut away all the different gods. But all the people who got missionarized by the missionaries of Christianity they themselves had a whole big, cosmic constellation of gods. For instance, the Germanic tribes they dealt with Odin, with Donar, with Holda. They had a lot of male and female gods, mostly living in the natural elements—in the fire, in the wind. These were not captured in figures like in the Greek antique culture. The Germanic symbol for all these living gods was mostly only a living tree nothing else. The people might apply some things to the tree, like a horse head, to stress a special god, but principally it was only like listening to the tree when the wind came in, or when the weather changed, or a rainbow came, or the moon appeared. You know, that is a kind of understanding of gods, which is not sculptured like in the antique world. It lives in the elements, and it belongs to all these different structures of gods: the gods in the earth, the gods on the earth, the upper and the lower nature, so, all the dwarfs, the elves, the fairies and these figures. And this was then cut away by the monotheistic principle that came from the Old Testament, through the New Testament and was carried out by the idea of Christianity. So, this is the mystery of the development of the world today. This has to be discussed all the time.

LAMA SOGYAL: Very much so. It is very interesting, in tantric Buddhism there is no God. You don't accept God, but yet there are gods.

BEUYS: I think, they must find the God in themselves.

LAMA SOGYAL: In themselves and also there are actually the energies that are possessed in spirits, like the land, and trees, and water, certain kinds of energy or, the element of the elements.

BEUYS: There is also the very old tradition in Tibet that comes from the animistic impulses of shamanism. What is it called?

LAMA SOGYAL: *Bön po.*

BEUYS: It was in the time before Buddhism came to Tibet. Are there still some characters like this existing in the present Tibetan philosophy?

LAMA SOGYAL: Yes, very much.

BEUYS: I was never there. But, I think, there must be some circles existing still, where one is very much directed towards this characteristic.

LAMA SOGYAL: Yes. I think, it is interesting that Buddhism is such a world of its own. In a sense, it embraces all not from the point of view of separateness but in a non-dualistic way. For instance, it is believed that, first of all, to relate to duality directly is the first non-dual understanding. It is very much: how to use duality to transcend it. For us to be non-dual in itself is very difficult. It is how to use duality in a certain way, which makes that sparkle, that non-dual experience. And so, it is from that point of view that everything is accepted—on that a lot of what you might call freedom, flexibility, depends.

If, suppose, one person relates to the truth in a certain way, then the teaching is applied in that particular person's way of thinking. For instance, there is a story of a thief, a very famous thief in India, who was very successful. He was very good at it, but then he got really bored with it. There was no longer any adventure, no fun at all. So, one day he failed and he got really disgusted. He then thought: "I must change my life. It is very sinful." He heard there was a very great yogi, a very great master, in the village. He went to visit him and said: "Master, I have sinned a lot. I have robbed people. I have to change my life. Would you please help me?"

So, the master asked: "What are you good at?" He said: "I am not good at anything." But the master said: "You must be good at something." Then he said: "Well, actually I am very good at stealing." The master said: "That's excellent. I want you to sit and steal all the stars and everything that you see. Steal them into your belly and dissolve them." The thief did this for about twenty-one days, then he began to realize that actually outer-perception is a manifestation. It is all the mind's projection. He began to realize that, in a very intrinsic way, in a very real way. And at that moment he realized.

BEUYS: Fantastic. I think, we should carry on with this idea.

LAMA SOGYAL: It is a very, very good idea. It's a wonderful idea.

BEUYS: And then we go to Beijing. There are a lot of other demands within the people of China. I think, it is a necessity to speak with the government. I think, the government should see that all the economical concepts are not highly developed. So, from the point of view of economy . . .

LAMA SOGYAL: Economy would be a very important thing.

BEUYS: Economy has to be the link with all the other dimensions. Economy is not only a money making principle. Economy is principally, from its own nature, a way of production to fulfill the demands of the people all over the world. Here the idea of democracy plays a very important role. The idea of democracy being related only to a kind of election system for political parties is nonsense. But justice in the production system, that is democracy. There democracy works with economy.

LAMA SOGYAL: The key to economy is confidence. There is a spirit of depression now, and there is an atmosphere of giving up. As a result you cannot stimulate.

BEUYS: Very difficult. But this relates to an idea of economy, which is only a false understanding of what capital means. They call capital the most important idea, but they don't relate the idea of capital to humankind's ability in work, they only relate the idea of capital to money. There is a completely false understanding of labor, productivity, and economy. For, a true economy has by its own natural character art in it because it belongs to the dignity, the creativity and the ability of the people.

LAMA SOGYAL: I think, that point might interest His Holiness the Dalai Lama—the economy and the social-political way.

BEUYS: Thanks to all the great spirits in the world, it is the result of our research to have found the organic unity of art and economy. The formula is: "Humankind's creativity is the capital." The money is not the capital; the money can work as an exchange bill.

LAMA SOGYAL: Exactly. That's true. If there is a confidence between human beings as people, then it could be . . . You see, the most important thing about economy is that it must circulate, pass hands. And if there is a confidence, then you are willing to give.

BEUYS: That is right.

LAMA SOGYAL: So that, I think, is where the real block is.

BEUYS: If we would lead all the discussion and cooperation that is going on in the world to the problem of economy, then the problems arising would never end in wars. Only the interference of political ideologies lead to wars. And so the ideologies have nothing to do with the reality. We are far away from the reality.

LAMA SOGYAL: Ideologies are protecting certain rights.

BEUYS: Are protecting power. Now, one has to speak about some very negative instincts in some people, who want to maintain personal power over other people. But, I think, there are a lot of reasons for believing that also in China we could look for a good understanding. I think, this vision contains a lot of truth.

LAMA SOGYAL: In Buddhism we have the karmic principle that: "If you give, you will receive." So, the best investment is to give.

BEUYS: Yes, sure.

LAMA SOGYAL: And again: "Give with the heart." The intention is very important. Giving with a certain intention really creates a kind of economy in a sense . . . a sound economy!

BEUYS: Yes, that is the basic law of all economics. The most important law for economy is: "The more you are producing for others—and do nothing else than thinking of other people, not trying to live off your production—then your needs for living are covered by the work of other people. You must not care for yourself, you must care for other people. And other people have to care for you."

LAMA SOGYAL: That is true. That is interdependence.

BEUYS: Yes . . . that is a basic law.

LAMA SOGYAL: Very, very important.

BEUYS: But it is not respected in our society so far!

LAMA SOGYAL: I think, that is very important. These are the things that should be really brought to people's attention. People should be reminded . . . people should be reminded of the basic principles of economy so as not to be lost.

BEUYS: Exactly.

LAMA SOGYAL: Because since it is the age of specialists, general things are left out. The fundamentals are left out because everything is left to experts. Therefore it is very important that such knowledge should come to the common people.

BEUYS: That's right. My other statement which I often make is, that every enterprise—also the industrial enterprise working with, let's say, metals, iron—has to get the character of a university at the same time, which means that the people, for a time, work with their hands on the resources. But the rest of the time they are working on the development of the capital which is no other thing than their own ability!

LAMA SOGYAL: That's very important. If you do that, you would perhaps not only produce good workers but you would also produce very good minds.

BEUYS: Sure. But without good minds, no good production!

LAMA SOGYAL: Yes, that is true. These things should be brought to people's attention and should be discussed with His Holiness. And it could be experimented, you know . . . tried out.

BEUYS: We are doing it as a model, as an enterprise model. Even though this enterprise model is small, it finds a lot of interest.

LAMA SOGYAL: I think, those kinds of things, like that you have put this to work as an experiment, these things would be very important for you to bring up with His Holiness.

BEUYS: Very fine, Lama Sogyal. Now I leave you and I hope we will see each other.

LAMA SOGYAL: We'll see each other soon—definitely.

Interview with Alan Moore
and Edit deAk
1974

ALAN MOORE: I was wondering, what kind of conception do you have of California? Can you describe it? Or just tell a story about California.

EDIT deAK: The idea is the myth of a foreign land.

JOSEPH BEUYS: I would be interested to be in California for a few weeks to make investigations in nature, botany, and animals, and the shore, and the fishes, and the streams to the sea, and all these things, yes; and the galleries and the dealers, and the mountains, the climate, the population. I am interested in the closeness to Mexico, and to see the difference between the character of this part of the United States compared with the East.

MOORE: How do you expect that people will respond to you?

BEUYS: I never had a bad response to the teachings. I am not so interested to just speak about art and the artist and the art scene.

I would try to come in touch with people from other fields: the scientist, the people in the streets.

MOORE: There's nobody on the streets in California. They all drive.

deAK: If you went to California and worked with an animal, what animal would you choose?

BEUYS: I would be further interested in the coyote and the desert animals mostly. California in my vision is an unclear country, really. It has not so much clear history. The only story I know about California is the Sutter story, the gold of Sacramento. The special element to me that is of curious importance is that when I go to California, it's the way to the West, yes, but in reality I reach the East. There the elements of West that we use, elements for culture and power and behavior, these things become turned in a way. If you stand in California on the coast—I never did it— and look to the west, in reality you look to the east. All these spiritual elements that come from this side are Eastern powers, cultural powers, nature powers, historical powers, the influence from the East. It's another thing. I live in Europe for instance. (*Draws map.*) Here's the Berlin Wall, yes, against Poland, Russia, Siberia, and all the East—Japan, Asia, and all this. When I look to the west, I come to the Netherlands, France, England. When I look from Germany to England, I see the incoming Western powers as I'm looking for creating the world of the future, developing all these ideas of the future from Western ideas, or you could say Middle European ideas. But when I come here, here's the border, here's the end of the United States, and I look to the west and I can't. Here it changes.

deAK: Do you think that the American Indians, their past, their life or their ideas, has to do with the East?

BEUYS: There is this problem of the coming together of the elements of the East and the West. I put it better a few years ago, and I cannot now find the real connections. But the evolution goes from the East. The Indians are in reality Asiatic people, but they changed almost their whole race elements in the Western area, and together with the powers of the land in America, they changed almost the whole biological substance, too. Therefore it is a special kind of secret how these Asiatic elements came over the Bering Strait long ago. It's the same with the coyote. When I worked with the coyote, I had the idea that it was not an indigenous animal. It came as a wolf with the Indians over the Bering Strait. And this Asiatic wolf, or stepwolf, changed his whole biological configuration and behavior. Then it was my idea to import the coyote once more back to Europe, and you could see it change back to the European wolf or Siberian wolf. It is a transformed European wolf, the coyote, how it came to the character of a brush wolf.

deAK: The coyote was a very important animal for the American Indians in pre-Columbian times. They are connected with a whole ritual of death. Then with the cowboys that all changed, because they saw the coyote differently.

MOORE: Chicken-killer.

Interview with Louwrien Wijers
1979

It is Thursday the 22nd November 1979. We are in the studio of Joseph Beuys, Drakeplatz 4 in Düsseldorf. In New York the exhibition of his work in the Guggenheim Museum opened on the 2nd of November and will be until the 2nd of January. In Rotterdam a show of his drawings opened on the 17th November at the Museum Boymans van Beuningen and will go until the 6th of January. In the last weeks of December Joseph Beuys will travel back to New York to lecture. On the 17th and the 18th of April 1980 Joseph Beuys will be going to Rotterdam to lecture. Our talk starts at 10:30 in the morning. There is a break to take lunch with his wife and his son and daughter in the new house near the studio that the family has moved into only two weeks before. The taping of this interview ends around 4:30 in the afternoon.

LOUWRIEN WIJERS: I wanted to start with your exhibition in the Guggenheim Museum. Can you tell what the show is like and how you feel about this retrospective?

215

JOSEPH BEUYS: The first necessity for this exposition was to get clear with this building. The building has no large spaces ranging to different directions, like, for instance, such a space as we are sitting in now. So since this building consists of only one way spiralling down alongside a wall, it gives for me not the possibility to show larger environments for instance. So I had to come to a kind of shaping of the exposition, to show in some constellation a kind of environmental character which is a very important part of my work. In reality, there is not an environment existing in its true meaning. So I had to find a constellation with sculptural knots, or I called them "stations." I made a concept running from the top to the ground floor consisting of twenty-four stations. These stations consist more of sculptural, environmental knots, one could say.

That was the first decision I made after having seen the building three years ago. I then made this concept and now, during the realization of this concept I found it was a very correct decision I made three years ago. So I had nothing to correct on this concept and I feel this is now an ideal constellation for the building, and also to give people a kind of overview over my work, over my intentions in my work. Nevertheless environmental work in its more special meaning does not exist there.

WIJERS: Which are the pieces shown at the stations?

BEUYS: I am speaking further. I want to say another dimension. Because another regulator for the character of this exposition was that the wish of the staff, especially of Thomas Messer, was to give such an insight in my work that it would also cover a kind of chronology, a retrospective also giving an insight for the people into the whole development of my work.

So "Station One" starts with a piece beginning in 1948 or 1947. So you get a kind of chronology. Also this works very fine in the building and in a way there is no compromise done in the thing. Nevertheless the thing is from the environmental point of view a kind of restriction of my work, one could say.

But a completion of the whole character of my work, showing all the dimensions is therefore done in the catalog. This catalog gives an overview over the complete character of intentions. Also the pedagogic intentions, the political intentions and the organizational intentions I included in the catalog, you see.

What is also a very good completion which I had never done before is to show sculptural characters of my work—spatial characters of my work—together with this drawing cycle "The Secret Block of a Secret Person." I never did like a mixture of drawings and a sculptural show, but now, for the first time, it fits very fine in the building and there is in no way a disturbance of drawings, sculptural things and so on. One could say more vice versa: it gives the people a kind of leading line, an insight in the themes of my work and the intentions, which are reflected sometimes also in the drawings. So it is not a theoretical introduction, I think. Each introduction has a character of images, therefore it is not necessary to give the people a kind of interpretation, because there is always a kind of connection between the drawings and the sculptural things.

So that led to this character of the building which is in fact a very transparent, open and easily to receive form.

WIJERS: Yes.

BEUYS: And so it found also a very positive echo, I think. Perhaps also because it is the first time the Guggenheim building is okay for art. I removed all fake walls, all ceilings which worked as a kind of decoration. I removed the blue pool-fountain and re-painted it white, as it was in the beginning and as it was planned also by Frank Lloyd Wright. I gave it back a very original, simple and sober character.

WIJERS: The architect must be happy.

BEUYS: Some people were saying: "When Frank Lloyd would have seen such a composition, such a presentation, he would have had nothing against art anymore", because Frank Lloyd Wright was not so much intended to have a kind of museum made out of this building. Some people say it was concepted for a garage originally.

WIJERS: Really.

BEUYS: And other people say, looking for architectural intentions, that perhaps Frank Lloyd Wright made a kind of monument for his own architectural intentions and did not stress the necessity of a museum showing sculptures, paintings and so on. Now this is what one could say in the first go about the workability in relation to the concept of the show. So I do think my decision was right to restrict also the number of pieces. I restricted the thing to twenty-four knot-positions, called stations, and I show there some tools coming from actions, existing there like documents of ac-tions. And together with an audioguide which everybody can get there . . .

WIJERS: With text by you?

BEUYS: Yes, I speak personally in this audioguide . . . and to-gether with the catalog, which a lot of people buy, and together with shortened descriptions of political ideas, which people can have, I think for half a dollar—it is a short description of the political ideas—I think it's possible to come to a very reasonable information about things.

WIJERS: How many drawings are there?

BEUYS: "The Secret Block" consists of about four hundred drawings.

WIJERS: And at the knots, the stations, what can one see there?

BEUYS: There is, for instance, a very sober, or one can say almost nothing, of a kind of sculpture: a divided cross in a cubic existence standing very simply on the floor. This gives the impression that there is a kind of end product of a larger action with some very complicated interaction and participating of public influences during the two days of the action. So sometimes there is only the end result, the kind of finale, to be seen of some very large action. This action is then described in the catalog, so people can have an impression of the dimensions of such a thing. (*Joseph Beuys opens up the Guggenheim catalog.*)

You see, this is the finale of a larger action. Only this stands very simple on the floor. But the whole action consists of a very lot of elements, you know. This box is, for instance, filled with fat and pumps, air pumps. Hundred kilos of fat and hundred air pumps. Nobody can see it. And there is also no special atmosphere. So there is a kind of problem for the people to reconstruct the meaning of the thing. You see, there is a lot of action implied, also with fire, with warmth, with light, with sound, participation of people. Yes, that is the special character of my work, and then, if you have the task to make an exposition, you can only show the finales, the end results, or the tools of some actions. Sure, there are a few sculptures which have their own meaning from a sculptural point of view, but this belongs more to my older work from the beginning, from the Forties, Fifties. So there we have then the fulfillment of a kind of chronology and development in my work.

(Leafing through the catalog again) You see, the catalog follows exactly the structure of the exposition. If you see, for instance, my beginning here, then one can see such a head of wood as a sculpture. These metal sledges also. And it starts with the bathtub here. Every station is marked by a full page image and a page with a kind of other color in the catalog. So when the people go through the catalog, being involved in the development of things, they can restrict their interest to the stations, because at the same time one can see the whole neighborhood of ideas and activities there.

So from Station One, "The Bathtub," to Station Two, this iron cage, there are to be seen some smaller sculptures of that time. And then in parallelity to this there are drawings in the background, also starting from 1943 or 1945, I don't know.

WIJERS: Even that early.

BEUYS: Yes, yes, even that early.

So now the next one is the third station and here comes already the history of the beginning of the actions. Here are some drawings of "The Secret Block" in the catalog. Also here. And here is Station Four. This is a period of sculptures which have their own meaning only as sculptures. Also these first fat and wax sculptures come now. They are not mentioned as stations, one can see them in showcases sometimes. Here is a drawing of "The Secret Block" in the neighborhood of such forms. Station Five. Some drawings of "The Secret Block" again. But here are not only drawings of "The Secret Block," here are also some drawings from other collections which have a kind of nearness to the intention of this sculpture.

WIJERS: Can you say something about "The Secret Block?"

BEUYS: "The Secret Block" is in my understanding one work. It is not a collection, like the collection one can see in Rotterdam now (drawings, watercolors and gouaches). My intention was to have it as a kind of book, as one work. So it has a consistency of themes in it. It has the idea of a history. And so I declared it years ago as one work, like an environment in a drawing character, which is never done before as far as I know. It does have a nearness to other real drawingbooks I made. I made for instance the Ulysses consequence in smaller books. So that drawingwork exists in drawing character in a book. But for "The Secret Block" every drawing has a special size, every drawing has a special color, there are oil colors used, watercolors used, pencil drawings, ink drawings, fat drawings and different materials. While the book conceptions I made, like the Ulysses, are all existing like books.

There is in "The Secret Block" a kind of spiritual idea of a history. One can look at it as a biography, or as a spiritual history being related to some, one could say, to some secrets because it is called: "The Secret Block for a Secret Person in Ireland." It has a relationship to Celtic intentions, also one could say to Indo-Eurasian-Germano-Celtic intentions. It is a kind of spiritual history, a kind of thinking model to bring out spiritual intentions that one could use immediately to develop another history. It is a model character to develop another history and therefore this work is very important, also for my political work.

WIJERS: It goes throughout the years?

BEUYS: Yes, it goes throughout the years. The first drawing, I think, starts in 1936 and it ends about 1970. About this time we have the last drawings. Have you never seen the catalog of "The Secret Block?" (*Joseph Beuys gets up and comes back with a copy of the catalog published by the Museum of Modern Art in Oxford in 1974.*) So that is "The Secret Block," you know. The cover shows a kind of political information I did during an action I made in Chicago. (*Quickly showing the content he hands the book to me.*) That is then for you.

(*At the same time he has brought in a series of six black books that he shows now.*) These are not separate drawings, this is a whole history in these books. This is never shown. There is a similar idea as in "The Secret Block." These were made in 1958 and perhaps 1959. This work consists of about 660 drawings, smaller intentions of ideas also showing a kind of theory of sculpture. One could make an analysis of this to come to a theory of sculpture. I think the theory of sculpture is very important, because on the basis of the theory of sculpture the whole political work is developed.

It is too much to look at all the drawings now. I show it only to give you an impression. (*Joseph Beuys brings back the six black books and sits down again.*)

WIJERS: Could you show enough items of your vast work?

BEUYS: I think there is enough. I think even one piece more would be perhaps too much. There is a good conversation of very small intentions, small results of sculptural doings, and also there are very big, more monumental characters of action-sculptures, like these twenty-four tons of fat.

I am not, I am really, really not keen principally on making such expositions, because they withdraw me from my actual work. This exposition took very complicated preparations. Just to make sure the problems of packing for instance, which is a very difficult thing sometimes, because the material is very flexible and is sometimes impossible to transport, like fat. So it took me half a year of my actual work. I had to make restrictions from my actual work. And I don't like things which are involved in my biography, which are involved in my work that I have already done.

WIJERS: That's the past.

BEUYS: It is the past, you know. So that is the problem. But I think, if one would make a kind of *"Bilanz"* (balance) now after the show, one could say: the output is bigger than the input. So it has a very positive result. It has also a very positive feedback to the situation here in Germany, because it works in a very fine way along with my political intentions. Now people understand the implications, the integration of art and social work. They understand more and more about the interdependency of what I understand as art and the social sculpture, so an understanding of art as being related to everybody and to every section, or every power field of our society.

So *Der Spiegel*, you know (*Joseph Beuys shows a copy of the German weekly magazine* Der Spiegel *with his picture on the cover.*) writes in a relatively correct way about the interdependency of political intentions, so-called political intentions, and what an enlarged understanding of art would mean. It is for the first time that a paper like *Der Spiegel* is interested to discuss this subject.

WIJERS: That is because for the first time, from a big museum outside Germany, you send such strong vibrations over the whole world.

BEUYS: Yes, this belongs to the output, to the positive results of such wonder circles. You know, I don't like wonder circles.

But I have a feeling that I will never do such a thing again, such a retrospective. Its final interest is the case of having people to cooperate in a museum sculpture, but, in fact, I am only interested in showing new work, new things. I am finished now with my biography, you see. At this time it was perhaps necessary, because the enthusiasm of Tom Messer and the people in the United States was very clear and on a very strong line of honesty. There was no underthought, no by-thought. It was a very clear intention of a wish to have this piece as a biographical overview over my intentions. So I think there was no reason to deny again a kind of exposition in this form.

WIJERS: When you say "deny again," do you mean this same question had often come to you?

BEUYS: Oh yes, from everywhere. For instance this exposition would have the possibility to go for years and years through the United States, because there are questions from, I think, almost twenty institutions in the United States and even from South America and Canada to have this constellation. And there are also questions from here, from Germany, to take over this whole exposition.

WIJERS: And from Japan?

BEUYS: Yes, they have a lot of interest, but they did not especially ask for this Guggenheim exposition.

WIJERS: Because in the Museum of Modern Art in Tokyo I saw many Beuys-copies, done by young Japanese artists.

BEUYS: I receive every day letters from Japan. There is a very intensive interchange of ideas. And young Japanese artists are very often coming. But I think the institutions are at the moment in Japan a bit flat.

But perhaps it depends on the difficulty to have such an exposition from my side, because very often I refused to do expositions in this style.

WIJERS: You realized this one and that will be it.

BEUYS: Yes, yes.

WIJERS: There was an exhibition at René Block's in Berlin not long ago?

BEUYS: That was not an exposition, that was an action. It was the action of tearing down the whole activity of René Block, because he finished his whole gallery work. And so I made this last action to clear down the walls of the gallery. It had a kind of dependency on the coyote-action; the coyote-action I did in the United States . . .

WIJERS: . . . in 1974 at René Block's gallery in New York.

BEUYS: Yes. So there were now some documents of this coyote-action in the gallery in Berlin. We decided to make the last action in relation to the coyote-action and we called this whole action: *"Ja, jetzt brechen wir hier den Scheiss ab."* That was the name: "Now let's tear down the whole shit." Then the trash from the walls was packed in crates and sent to the United States. And there is now exhibited this trash of the Berlin situation in the Feldman Gallery, and there it has the title: *"Aus Berlin: Neues vom Kojoten."* So there is the whole trash now in the Feldman Gallery as a parallel activity to the Guggenheim show, so people can see also then the last environment I made; in parallelity to the retrospective in the Guggenheim.

(*Joseph Beuys gets up and comes back with a booklet bearing the title* "Aus Berlin: Neues vom Kojoten," *published by Block and Feldman.*) This is a fine book showing the idea. It gives in a way the history of the Block Gallery. It was done by Feldman and René in cooperation. (*Then pointing at pictures of piled up crates.*) Here is the whole trash of the gallery. (*Turning over the pages*) Here is the gallery now finished. Here René Block. Everything is now already crated, and all this stuff is down so you can really see what kind of place this was. (*Reading aloud:*) "It's about time that somebody said where culture's happening—it's not happening in Mies' Museum"—that is the National Gallery— "It's happening right here." That was this environment, this activity with tearing down and I made there some very well-known features of my work; fat corners. Here is, for instance, a filter-fat corner. Here is a fat wedge. Also here. So everything is down now. These are residues from the coyote-action. This is a piano from another action I made in Berlin. Also these (*hat with hole and music stand*) are pieces from actions you know. There is the loudspeaker from which every minute it sounds: "*Und nun brechen wir hier den Scheiss ab.*" Here objects of the Karl-Marx-Platz-action that I made in Berlin seven years ago. Here is a kind of video information on the wall about this action with the sweeping (on Karl-Marx-Platz). These are the pieces of the coyote-action, the residues. This is torn felt. There is the *Wall Street Journal*. Fat corner. *Wall Street Journal*. That is hair of the coyote and my own hair and two nails, my own two nails. But this constellation is in another form. (*A new chapter called "The Plaster" starts so Joseph Beuys remarks:*) And here is the history of all the actions which took place in Berlin; different actions.

WIJERS: How many crates with trash went over?

f.

BEUYS: I think there were about sixty crates. It is a kind of mountain in the gallery . . . (*While speaking he keeps turning the pages and interrupts himself.*) This were all activities in Berlin. The sweeping of Karl-Marx-Platz. Here again are some samples of the coyote-action. That is a piece I did in London and Berlin and New York ("*Richtkräfte,*" 1974). That is the documenta (1977). That's a concert I did for Maciunas. ("In memoriam George Maciunas, *Klavierduett* Joseph Beuys & Nam June Paik.") It's in the Academy (in Düsseldorf). There is Nam June Paik. Pictures of the last action. Here you can also have this. (Joseph Beuys gives the book to me.)

WIJERS: Then there is Rotterdam. Except for the drawing-show now there are meetings scheduled. What are your plans for Rotterdam?

BEUYS: This depends on the activity of the people in Rotterdam. I am really open for every kind of activity. I've already made some proposals for how I could make a kind of up-to-date activity, finding a kind of association with the technical universities and other institutes existing in Rotterdam, to bring out this whole idea of an enlarged understanding of art, of an anthropological understanding of art and showing the idea what the Free International University means. We have made already a kind of plan for the beginning of the next year, a kind of activity then in the springtime, and a next action after the summertime. So that perhaps there can come up a kind of permanent cooperation between the Free International University and such an institute as the Boymans van Beuningen.

So that's an open future, you know. There is not a kind of dead decision for an activity standing in the museum's exposition plan. That's not how it is done. It is not even clear when exactly the first lecture, or discussion, or organized impulse will take place. You see it on the poster, there is described that there is a speech around the springtime and around the summertime. And it is completely open how long this first appearance would be; it could be only one or two days, or it could be perhaps a week of interdisciplinary activities. It is also open how much other workshops could participate in this thing.

I think that's a very good thing, and a very good idea, because everything is in change today. The traditional understanding of art is in a way flat, you know. But like all connections, or junctions, to a broader understanding of art, also the being open to a kind of social change, depends—especially when it deals with another country like the Netherlands, or England, or Northern Ireland—on the will of the people who are living there. I cannot just come with my ideas and say: let's make, I want to make, I will make . . . So I hear what the wants of the people there are, and if they want to do it, then I come. Because what is necessary to do here in Germany is not the same in the Netherlands. Every country has its own problems, its own needs, its own spiritual condition, and so one has more to hear than to act. One has more to be open for what is going on there.

WIJERS: Do you feel there is some inspiration for you in Rotterdam, some question or want?

BEUYS: All over the world one can find a kind of atmosphere which is intended to deal with new cultural forms. In Italy, for instance, I found a lot of resonance. So we founded there three institutes for the Free International University, or four now already; in Torino, in Pescara, in Roma and in Palermo. There are already people working in kinds of workshops, who are being confronted with the idea of what the Free International University wants to introduce, and wants to discuss in connection to the whole problem of humankind's life and of humankind's problems with their own—what one calls sometimes in a fashionable way—creativity, which means in reality the problem, or the question, of the freedom. How the question of the freedom could produce a human world in all different fields, beginning from the very important institutions like universities, schools, museums, and the whole cultural structure functioning in the field of democratic questions in the state, the understanding of the state and the law configuration, and the theory of having through the democratic regeneration of the constitutions an effect on the economical questions, being then related to the money system, to the bank system, and to, what people call the capital problem; the problem of the capital. And for this work of art, being engaged in the complete radical change of the social structure, one needs in fact a kind of very high developed philosophy and ways of production in the field of art—this art is then related also to objects, to drawings, paintings, sculpture, theater, happenings, actions, performances and everything that can be done in this character. But forerunning should be a kind of clear prospect on how things should, or have to change.

So it is therefore a psychological problem, a kind of consciousness problem; a problem of the thought. And therefore the logic of the thing, in my understanding is, that everything has to start with the thought, and that one has to look at the thought as an artist looks at his sculptural productions. So everything depends on the quality . . . everything depends on the quality . . . So already the thought is under the scrutiny of the quality. And so this interdependency of ideal thinking powers, speaking powers, molding powers, until it reaches the impact on the condition of the capital, the money, that is, I think, a very gigantic work.

And that is what I call the Social Sculpture. Very often misunderstood. And very often described as an utopian idea, but it is in fact no other thing than what we need every day.

WIJERS: Do you find there is a good thinking quality for you to work with in Holland?

BEUYS: Yes, but I do not start in the beginning with the idea of quality. In the beginning one has not to put the question of quality, in the beginning one has to look for the interest of the people. If there is not the interest and the will of the people to discuss these things, then there is not a reason to start with a kind of process. No, I speak about the quality when the process is through, is done, and has ran through its course after a special time. No, one has to start with the quality one finds. And perhaps sometimes there is no other thing than a misquality in the beginning.

So I am not an eliterian person. The whole problem cannot be solved with the kind of eliterian positioning of looking only for quality, because the whole world is a misquality. Therefore one has to start with the condition one finds in special situations, and then, in the first grade of development it deals only with some amelioration, with some betterments in the engagement of the people, the interest of the people. But it has also . . . in this kind of development that runs through steps of amelioration, it is, at the same time, always in comparison with the meaning of the quality, of the highest quality humankind could produce for its own life and even more than life, you know. So it is a kind of beginning in the first go, and then there appears very often a kind of struggle between very hard shapes, constellations in humankind's psychology, very hard believers in ideologies. For instance, Marxist meanings one has to discuss. And one has not to fear a kind of resistance and even not to fear the enemies of the idea.

So, it has to develop a big catalog of qualities already in the beginning. One has, for instance, to be fearless against what could happen from the enemies of humankind towards such a plan. There are existing a lot of wasters of the land and wasters of humankind's existence now in the political structure of the two capitalistic systems; of this Western private capitalistic system and this state bureaucratic monopoly system in the East, running along ideologies with Marxistic philosophies like dialectic materialism, historical materialism, and believers in such a kind of, what they call, socialism.

So this has to start and is already on a very good line of development. Here in Germany, even my organizations I founded in 1967 and I founded in 1970 and I founded in 1972, show now the first very interesting results. In the meantime, already in almost every daily paper, one can read about what the meaning of the Green Movement, the ecological movement, is. So there is a thought now existing in the system, in this case, for a big part due to the ecological movement, in which our Free International University is highly involved as the advising workshop for the whole making of programs, and for the whole strategy and tactics.

So there exists a thought in the system which can never be leveled with the system. This, for instance, is a very important thing especially where it deals not only with the outer, parliamental activities, but also with the parliamental methods to compete, for instance in the elections, with the system. This has already started during the European Parliamental Election with the very good result of three-and-a-half percent of the voters in West Germany, but we have to care for more. We have to reach the five percent hurdle, then we could deliver some people in parliaments. This is the constellation for the federal election, for the federal parliament, but as far as other parliaments, lower parliaments in districts, are concerned, we have already delegates in such parliaments. And we eat already very sharp the Liberal party here. Also the Liberal party is almost on the 5 percent hurdle, so perhaps the Liberal party disappears during the next election. And perhaps the Social Democratic party gets weakened, and also the Christian Democratic party gets weakened by the effect of the voter's decision to go in another direction, to deal with a very human ideal, to deal with an ecological ideal and to deal with an ideal of human being and nature.

WIJERS: In the conception you strive for.

BEUYS: In this conception I was already speaking about; that everything of society has to be transformed. And as more people are interested to transform it, and as more people see how it could be transformed, then there is really the possibility to transform it. Also this transformation is not even a complicated one. When one sees this more and more people will acclaim and will follow such a development. So I see there is no way to stop such a kind of impulse.

Perhaps there is a kind of hinderance appearing in the future, but then our task has to be, to bring the people better information, or even a better formulation of what their own need is.

WIJERS: What hinderance do you expect?

BEUYS: There is very often a kind of psychological hinderance dealing with the old fashioned constellations. And there is perhaps the intention in people that they are wondering if it would not be necessary to vote again for the Social Democratic party to avoid this Franz Joseph Strauss from coming up. But in fact there is no problem. Some people think there is a problem.

There is no difference in reality between the Christian Democratic party and the Social Democratic party. There seems to be a difference, but there is no difference. Both parties have no difference in their meaning about how the system should run. The difference is only in how they work to get central power in the state. There is the difference. But we are against this centralism.

WIJERS: When you go to America for lectures will this be your subject there too?

BEUYS: Yes, sure. It was already my subject in the lectures I did years ago in Minneapolis, and Chicago, and New York, and in other places. It is exactly the same theme and it is perhaps now in another constellation, so that we can bring in now further ideas, further developed ideas. And we can already bring in a kind of experience. We can speak about facts, how they run here, daily facts. We can report that this idea which I formulated years ago in the United States, has concrete, real results on the social body here. So we can report about results. That is the advantage of the lectures today, that we can speak about real constellations which were brought up by the impulse of this idea, coming also from different fields of initiatives.

WIJERS: Where are the lectures going to be this time?

BEUYS: They may be restricted to New York. I think one will be in a kind of open place, where people are involved in a kind of experimental workshop, that is called P.S. 1. And perhaps in another place called the New School. And another lecture will be maybe in the Guggenheim, if the people are still interested to

have such a lecture in the Guggenheim. The Guggenheim concept was to have a discussion with an American scientist, who is
involved in this field. That is the idea, and then towards the end
of the discussion it is planned to take the people into the discussion and have a kind of open discussion on the problems of art
and social body; the interrelationship of an anthropological understanding of art and the social body.

WIJERS: Do you think there is an interest for this in New York
now; will there be an open ear for what you say?

BEUYS: An open ear is always to find in the United States. There
is, I find, in the United States always the very good situation that
the people are interested. But the next position is another thing.
Perhaps there is a kind of weakness in the American society
regarding the evolving of ideas. They are very open and very
interested to hear about different things, but they are interested
in so many things that this gives a kind of confusion. Perhaps
they do not have the necessity to go to the root question of things;
to concentrate on a special idea.

In the United States very often you find an interest for very
different impulses, for Buddhistic things, for Zen Buddhistic
things, for Marxist things, for so-called open universities—what
they call open—for woman's liberation things. There are in
parallelity so many different things. And you find that for everything the people are open, and interested, and very nicely behav-
ing, and very friendly towards the idea. But sometimes I wonder
if this society is able to find this special one point where one has
to put the problem. Because there are not infinite possibilities to
start with this thing. There is only one point you can start with,
that is the idea of real creativity and the capital.

(Here Joseph Beuys gets up and prepares another coffee, while speaking about the enormous concentration of work in the past year. When the recording of the conversation starts again, he is saying:) It was a very hard time. Last year was terrible. So many problems, different problems, family problems, house problems, building problems, reconstruction of the academy space, then the Free International University, the European election, the Guggenheim exposition . . . It was terrible.

WIJERS: Is it a little bit better now?

BEUYS: A little bit better, but next year the federal election starts. That will be a very important conference. And then I have to move, then I have to go and speak in almost every German university.

Now I work a lot together with Rudi Dutschke. He is in a relatively good condition. He had a shot in his head during the Students Movement, but he recovers relatively well. And also I work with Bahro, Rudolf Bahro. He was in prison in East Germany. He was a critisist of the system in East Germany so he went to prison for two years. As soon as he came out, he fled to West Germany and now he is here in Cologne.

WIJERS: Is it possible for you to deal with European and American culture in the same way?

BEUYS: There is no difference. Yes sure, there is a difference, but from the political point of view there is not so much a difference because both belong to the same system: the private capitalistic system. The model of what is taking place in West Germany is exactly the American understanding of money and economics. West Germany is exactly the mirror of the American culture.

And you know about the influence of the German politics on Dutch politics through the European Market politics. Therefore there is no difference.

In a way one could say that America does not exist; that is the other consideration. Perhaps one time America starts to begin with its own idea, but the more I look at the situation, the more it seems to be a very, very European intention in the United States. With some differences and that's, for instance, the racism problem, that is another thing; that does not exist here in Germany. But all the other cultural conditions are relatively the same problems.

There is no difference. Perhaps a kind of mentality difference. In America this openness and this interest one can find sometimes in a better condition than here in Western Europe. But on the other hand everything goes quicker here. I find that in the United States everything goes very slow, very slow . . . There is no passion behind the ideas. I think there is perhaps an undescribable difference, but I would determine it in the positive way in saying that there is a very fine kind of really, really good people, and there is a very fine openness and interest in the things. But I wonder about the possibility for these people to focus and to concentrate on the only level from where one can change things. This broadness of interest perhaps hinders them to focus on the one point from where one can transform these things. That is the difference as far as I experienced the situation there.

So there I feel here in Europe more passion in the discussion, more fire in the thing, and more quickness. Therefore in comparison, through this quickness and through this drive things have reached here now, in a way, a relatively high vitality, and that does not exist there in this constellation. So I feel that the most important things which will take place in the next five or ten years, will take place here in Middle Europe. In Germany, the Netherlands, Denmark, England, Belgium, France perhaps, Italy, perhaps even East Germany . . . there will appear the next transformating step. So to my estimation there will be a change in the total organization of things, so in the places of production for ability goods, for creativity goods, for all abilities therefore, and in the places for the problem of the constitution, the democratic production places and the economical production places. There will take place some very intensive criticism on the existing institutions and partly a transformation. So I think these very important historical steps which humankind has to do on the recreation of the very ill constellations of society will take place in Europe. That is how I estimate the situation in comparison . . .

But I must admit, I don't know the rules of the constellation in the United States. I inserted only some kinds of thorns on different places. I have already my experiences with lectures in Chicago, Minneapolis and New York years ago, and now again I have some experiences there. But I feel even more, also thinking of my appearance there now, that changes will take place here in Middle Europe. That's what I feel.

WIJERS: There are no Free International Universities in the United States?

BEUYS: No, no. When there is a kind of interest between the people, then they will do it. There is a kind of very, very small workshop which calls itself Free International University and Artists' Cooperation, but I don't feel that from there the development of the idea of the Free International University will spread out. At the moment Caroline Tisdall, who wrote the catalog for the Guggenheim retrospective, is making a lecture tour through the United States. She is a member of the Free International

University and she will report after the tour about the constellations there.

WIJERS: She is very powerful it seems.

BEUYS: Yes, she is very powerful. She writes also in the political pages in *The Guardian* now. She will maybe report again and then we will know if there is a kind of interest in the Free International University; to organize the interest, because there is interest. I know there is interest. But perhaps there is a lack of will to realize the thing, because to realize is another work than to have interest. The realization brings a lot of work; a lot also of daily work, you know, which is not every day a very sensational feeling. It's a very hard work to do, daily work. I cannot care for the Free International University in the United States. I must concentrate now here on this situation and that is already almost too much for me to do every day; to do the things every day in a very good way. We cannot make all over the world workshops, or institutions, of the Free International University with the wish of these people that I am responsible for the things. If they really follow their own intentions, then it's okay. But it must not be a thing—that would be again a kind of misunderstanding—where my person has a function in the thing. Only the idea is the thing. It has nothing to do with personalities. There is no difference in value between the person who is caring for the space here in Düsseldorf, and a person like me. Sometimes people think that the Free International University is a Beuys-thing. But it has nothing to do with me. I founded it, yes sure, but that is the only thing. I founded it, but now I am only a member like every other member in this enterprise.

WIJERS: People have to carry it themselves.

BEUYS: Yes sure. Everybody can do it everywhere. Every time, everywhere people can do it, if they want to do it. Then perhaps it has a special value to take up contact with us and use all the experience we had already during the years. And they can reread all that we gave out as information. Surely that would be okay, but we cannot organize from here a kind of place in the United States. That's impossible. It is against the idea. There cannot appear a kind of hierarchy, or hierarchic structure. There cannot be a kind of leader. There can be only a kind of free membership in the enterprise. And as far as the rights are concerned, everybody has the same rights, and duties, to fulfill.

WIJERS: One works on one's own inspiration.

BEUYS: Exactly. That's right. But what is a very interesting thing: some connections with the United States one has to see perhaps in a new light. For instance, for some people perhaps it appears as a kind of nonsense that, for instance, already even Andy Warhol is interested in what is going on here with the Green Movement, the ecological movement. And perhaps Andy Warhol will participate in the election campaign in West Germany next year. Perhaps it would be a very nice picture to have Rudi Dutschke and Andy Warhol and me, and some other people, perhaps some philosophers of the German sociology on the theme. It would be a very good thing.

WIJERS: Did you see Andy Warhol in New York?

BEUYS: Yes, I saw him there and I saw him here.

WIJERS: And he is enthusiastic?

BEUYS: Yes, in a way. He has his own understanding of enthusiasm.

(Joseph Beuys takes a triptych print from the table and hands it to me.) That was this action with Andy Warhol here in Düsseldorf. *(The giant invitation reads: "Joseph Beuys, Robert Rauschenberg, Andy Warhol; exhibition 7 November till 5 December 1979." It shows a silkscreen by Robert Rauschenberg, a silk screen by Andy Warhol and a photograph of Joseph Beuys.)* I made the action in two places. One in the Galerie Schmela, and one in the Galerie Mayer.

WIJERS: And Robert Rauschenberg was there too?

BEUYS: No, no, no. I did not see Rauschenberg. He couldn't come. He apologized for not being there. It was meant for the three of us. But he couldn't come . . .

(Some time later we talked on the telephone about the progress of the collaboration with Andy Warhol in the election campaign.)

BEUYS: I saw Andy twice since November last year and I will meet him now in April in Italy on a political event in Naples, two days. We must see. It is always difficult to deal with Andy Warhol on a political level.

(The interview continues with the subject Vienna, where Joseph Beuys was offered a seat as professor at the academy.)

WIJERS: How is your situation with Vienna now?

BEUYS: I refused to take this professorship in Vienna. I felt there was a kind of demand in a very old fashioned way. The kind of work they offered I did already twenty years ago. But I do have a very good relationship to some persons there, and also to the school. So now I have a free contract. It means that I appear as often as I can and have meetings with the students, speaking about the problems of the art. Also I have a possibility to establish the Free International University in Vienna. So it comes now more along the line of some new ideas, whereas the other thing was more a getting again involved in a state enterprise, in a state university.

WIJERS: I was told that you were even going to move to Vienna.

BEUYS: No, no. I had never in mind to move there.

WIJERS: Now the subject "mysticism." Reviews on your show in the Guggenheim Museum say that the people over there are especially attracted by the mysticism in your work. In the *Soho News*, art critic John Perrault writes that you bring a totally new feeling to America with this mysticism that your work has. How do you look at that mysticism yourself?

BEUYS: There is no mysticism. The first distortion of the idea is that it deals with mysticism. Perhaps there is some mystics in it, but not mysticism. And there is a difference between mystic and mysticism.

I don't know what they call mysticism, it is in truth perhaps the interest of the spirit; that the work expresses the spirit, and not the formal aspect. While in the United States a lot of art production runs along the line of formalistic art; what one could call the postmodernism, a kind of formalistic intention like Don Judd, Carl Andre, Robert Morris and these things. The people make a kind of equation between the European impulse in this moment in my work, and they feel a real other intention to go on with art, an intention which is related to the problems of the world and related to the questions existing on ecology and on powers, you know. My work is mostly related to creative powers. Whereas the American intentions go more—I must repeat—along the formalistic aspects of the things. That's what the critics also say often, that there lies the difference.

The people feel perhaps, even from such an exposition which is there as a kind of retrospective—not the best constellation to transform the idea—but they feel from the objects, that the objects have to do with a real other context; that this context is variated to all directions, to the existing problems of human-kind—nature, society, psychology, creativity. The existing questions have to bring up the consciousness and then the consciousness has to be researched again and has to be brought up to a real other, higher level of understanding what culture means. That they feel. And I think they quote it sometimes with the word mysticism. But there is perhaps not a clear consciousness on the differences of mysticism and mystics and spirit and conscious-ness. I think that's perhaps the excuse for the application of the word mysticism in the intentions of the writers. So I refuse to be ever interested in mysticism.

But, you know, everything in nature, every tree, every animal has its own mystics, its own secrets, which aren't solved until now, which are not even considered in our present civilization with a materialistic, polytheistic understanding of science and art. So I stress the necessity to change the understanding of science and art and to broaden the idea of points of reality. My reality is another reality than the reality of the American modern art.

WIJERS: It seems American people have a hunger for your reality.

BEUYS: Yes, sure. American people are conditioned for the spirit. How could it be otherwise, because also the American people are people, the same people as our people; principally they are people. And they are longing for spirit. That's the problem. They are longing for living in a kind of reality, whereas they are feeling that it isn't reality, where they are living now. That it's a kind of distortion and destroying of the real reality of life possibilities. And they feel—they must feel—that they are in a way very unproductive; that this cannot lead to the free productivity of humankind, with the consequences of being able to find the solution for all the problems existing. So that again has to do with a kind of radical other energy impulse; or the plug is connected on a real other point. They plug the things on an opposite understanding sometimes, or very often.

WIJERS: Then they see where you plug in and they feel inspired!

BEUYS: Yes, in a way they are inspired. A lot of people came to me and congratulated me. Only by looking at the objects they felt something. And that works better in America than in Europe, because—I said it already—this openness in feeling is better developed in America than here. Here the people have very often reflections on: "What does that mean?" They are asking for a kind of literal, or philosophical excuse. Whereas the people in America look at the object and have a kind of radiation, they feel the radiation. That is better developed in the United States. They can read from the phenomenon. That, what I feel, is better developed and therefore the American public is a very fine public; they have possibilities and creativity in looking at constellations.

WIJERS: The hunger is more.

BEUYS: Yes, there is a hunger.

WIJERS: People here in Europe can still go into details with your work, whereas the Americans immediately receive the whole thing, because they need any inspiration for their survival.

BEUYS: Exactly. That is perhaps the meaning of this exposition in the Guggenheim; that there will come up a kind of discussion on very valuable cultural, basic thoughts. That is perhaps why it was done. And I had already a report from people who stayed much longer in the Guggenheim that every day it is very full. And there is even queuing in front of the museum. They must sometimes shut the doors, because of overflooding of the spiral there. I don't know, but I think it must depend on what you said; there must be a kind of hunger for these questions.

WIJERS: Can you say a bit more about what "mystic" means to you?

BEUYS: Yes, mystic means the undeclared secrets of life. But I do not call it mystics. I call it the unsolved questions in the whole culture. There we have a kind of culture which is only interested and able to develop material conditions—only to exploit the material conditions, to exploit the resources of the earth, and along with this to exploit also the humankind ability for a kind of profit, you know. For a kind of profit for very few, very mighty personalities and institutions. This means the problem of the state and the money. And one can take this already as a kind of international dilemma. All over the world this is principally the same, exploitations after the materialistic understanding of life. To exploit everything. While in comparison with this I am speaking about the necessity to enlarge the materialistic understanding to a kind of enlarged understanding of science, which would reach other questions existing.

So I speak about the necessity to enlarge the materialistic civilization-idea with other ideas. Then we can come to a more universal understanding of science and art. Then it would fulfill the need for an anthropological understanding of science and art.

So then it would take out of every question existing the spiritual question, and not the material condition as a problem where everybody can number, can rate, and can tell the profits out of these things. Then the profit can only be a kind of profit for humankind's development towards a much higher level of self-consciousness and culture. This stands in the middle of the question of man. What is the goal of humankind's life? What is the sense of humankind's life? And to give them this sense, or to give them this sense back, or to give a new sense to the people in the form of a germ towards a future much richer than every past, this gives the people a kind of power, and a kind of vitality, and a kind of ability in spirit, to transgress the borders of a restrictive civilization-idea, existing in the center. And surely then appears the idea of the repressive centralism. So it is to transgress and to transform the idea of what the capitalistic systems have done to the people.

WIJERS: We know of times that humanity was spiritually very evolved, now we are materialistically very evolved, and the future will be the unification, because we need to have both.

BEUYS: We need both, surely, we need both. I am not a regressive type, also there is very often a kind of misunderstanding. People who say: "Ah, this Beuys will go back to the Middle Ages, or to the stone dwellers, cliff dwellers." No, there is a misunderstanding. I have nothing against the materialistic methodology of analytics, but I think we have to enlarge this thing, not to get caught in a very restricted one-sidedness in our way of looking towards life. Because the problems of life, soul, humankind's spirit, the problems of intuition, imagination and inspiration, the problems of birth and death, the problems of survival in a bigger shape, and to bring in the image of the meaning of man, this can never be solved from a materialistic understanding of science. So I stress again the necessity to maintain the powers which the materialistic understanding of the world brought to humankind's mind. I am speaking for enlarging the scale, enlarging the circle of aspects. So I will only say we need more aspects. In a way very simply, or very traditionally one could say: We need the interdisciplinary discussion on the problems of life, and spirit, and nature.

WIJERS: But you are not so fond of people going to the East for spiritual development, who abandon their Western materialistic values . . .

BEUYS: No, that is no solution. That is the kind of underground culture and what we need is a kind of overground culture. We need not to creep into the caves, and in other mentalities, very high developed cultures of the past. This is already living in our abilities. We have to go after the lines of our logic in steps. So we have only to see that the materialistic understanding of the world has a lot to do with the idea of Christianity. To reach the earthly conditions and to get incarnated in this death, in this idea of the death, and that only from this, having really understood this impulse of the materialism, that there can only be a resurrection to have it clear with all the lines of the development.

But I have respect for people who are interested in what the Buddhistic style of philosophy has to tell. Sure, but I do not see a solution. At least I can say that there cannot be the methodology of the Western world to develop a spiritual world.

WIJERS: Do you see one line in the development of cultures in the world, and do you see the interconnection of spiritual leaders, with Krishna being related to Christ, who is so far the last of a sequence of spiritual masters?

BEUYS: Yes, for me Christ was surely the last of the spiritual masters, but especially this spirit, this Christ spirit, was related to the development of the idea of analysis in the world. And the development in this culture-step took place in the Western world therefore, more than in the Eastern world.

WIJERS: But you can see the whole world as one culture, in which the last master came more to the Western part.

BEUYS: Yes, that is true. But he did not come to the Western world, he was understood by the Western world. Surely he was for everybody, but he was understood, he was taken by the spirits of the Western world. So the root-fate of the Western world, starting at this moment, in parallelity to intentions which came also from other cultures—you have only to look at Apollo in Greece, there is a similar understanding of the idea of Christ; in Apollo is appearing a kind of *Vorgänger* (predecessor) for this Christ idea. So it is no wonder that at the same time when Christ appears, or almost at the same time, that then a methodology outcoming from the Greek culture is working with analysis. For instance, Aristoteles, rooting with one part of his geneality in the methodology of the old Greek culture, is with the other part of his ability directed towards the analytic way of the Western man. And so the whole range of philosophy throughout the Western world shows more and more the analytic way to reach a material consciousness to come to death, like Christ.

So there is a kind of repetition of this *mysterium* of Christ which took place in the Western world, and which ends with the fact that we have a materialistic understanding of the world. So because of this spiritual declaration of the material intention, the whole materialism is a spiritual thing. But when the people have too little power to overlook this methodology in the Christian impulse, they go back to a kind of Oriental methodology. That is, for instance, what in the churches is existing, the repetition of an almost Oriental right, with no idea how to declare Christianism.

WIJERS: Our interview last year had to end when you are saying that the mission of Christianity is to overcome death.

BEUYS: Yes, that's good. But first we have to make clear the problem of death and that is the mission of the methodology of materialism. So first the people have to die in a way, have to feel what death means, what a Buddhistic philosophy did avoid to reach the earth. There was an escape from the earthly conditions, to go to the spirit generally and principally. So this was one state in humankind's consciousness. But Christianity stressed a much more complicated system of development. In this way it means the dialectic system in its highest state of sense, while every other kind of understanding of dialectic systems distorts this principally dialectic complicated system of what Christianity means for humankind's transformation towards the spirit.

WIJERS: Can you explain how, in this frame, you look at death.

BEUYS: Yes, death belongs to life, you know. In the spiritual meaning life is not possible without death. That's again this kind of mystic, but it is not a mystification, because this mystic is experienced by everybody. Everybody can look through this constellation of powers. So again it deals only with the constellation of powers and energies in the world. But the people have to have and to develop another understanding than the materialistic understanding, which is only looking for powers that one can exploit with a distorting and debasing understanding of energies.

WIJERS: Could one say that to overcome the material way of thinking is to surpass the death of material things by adding its spirituality to it. When one has a material thing like a package of cigarettes lying on the table, one can look at it in a material way, but going beyond that you see that it is alive; it has a spiritual content too. And to be able to see that is to surpass death.

BEUYS: Yes, that is right. One could agree with that. But perhaps this package of cigarettes is not such a very convincing example. It is too complicated, because this package of cigarettes belongs in a way to another problem of the world. It is a good, produced by humankind's creativity. So it is a commodity. Surely there are materials involved in this thing, paper consists of wood and is developed of pulp, tobacco is produced of plants.

But better would be to see the problem by looking at the earth. If one looks at the earth, that everybody is standing on, one sees that the earth consists of minerals, substances like sands, and granites, and chalks—different minerals, you know. And this is the last materialization of the spirit, one could say. Nevertheless it is a very hard materialized condition; it means spirit. But it means a kind of death, then the whole spirit comes to an end. But this is not for all times. This is only a kind of fixation in a death-condition, and one can surpass it, one can recreate it, one can lead it back towards life.

So, for instance, agriculture has a lot to do with this problem. While a materialistic understanding which thinks that it would be a possibility to relabor this soil with artificial fertilizers, means only to add to this death-existence of the mineral another kind of mineral, which adds again the death-principle to death. So this will not lead to a regeneration of life in the fields. So already the problem of agriculture would mean, how to give life to the earth, how to bring spirit to the earth; only with spirit you can grow cabbages and potatoes.

WIJERS: If one can see that the earth is alive, then also one can see that this simple package is alive. God is in everything.

BEUYS: Yes, that is true, really it is true. But one has not to jump too early from the problem of the death-condition or the materialized aspect of the earth. Otherwise one would jump too quick over this problem. One must consider first that the earth is dead. It is already in a way dead from the beginning of the evolution of the earth. But then humankind was giving death to death and added every death-article to death-principles. And so that is the problem of agriculture; that is one specification of the whole problem.

So now it is dead, the earth is dead. But now, how can this death be surpassed, how can it be renewed, or regenerated. This depends on humankind's responsibility. There is no other spiritual being to do this work. Only people can do it. And this charges humankind with the total responsibility for the fate of the earth and for humankind's possibility for life on earth, you know. That is the meaning of why I said: "Let's not jump too quick over this death-problem." Death is a reality; it is a reality. And every day, what the international power is producing is death to death. Again death. Again death. Even harder, even better death, even more pollution, even more destruction, you know. And therefore humankind has to stand up, or rise, against this impulse. There is a possibility for humankind's development. And this is the secret, or this mystery, or this mystic, existing in Christianity, or in the impulse of Christ.

Sometimes people are not intended to distinguish between Christianity and what the churches did to the world. But the churches for me mean the same thing as political party organizations. Churches are organizations for central power, to take over the whole power. Also the new Pope is very clever in regaining the whole power all over the world. He is very clever in seeing that the governments are no longer able to take the power. Now he wants to regain the power which the papistry had already in the Middle Ages. So therefore he is a very danger for humankind. That's what I feel. People have to get clear with their mind and with their consciousness not to believe in what the Pope is saying. That is for me very important.

WIJERS: Although one always sees that above the level of institutions the real work is being done. So we must put our faith in the few free persons who can really think clearly.

BEUYS: Everything depends on the people. Everything. We have no right to shift the blame on political persons by saying: "He is guilty, the leader." No, everything depends on us. Therefore there exists only this necessity to see that everything depends on us, and that we can do it. Very easily we can do it. It's not so difficult to do. The whole power exists with the people. But if the people do not use their power, then the regressive powers will get bigger.

WIJERS: How is the overcoming of the death symbolized in Jesus Christ?

BEUYS: It is not symbolized. It is real. It is not symbolized. If you come in a space with a big flame of fire you will get burnt, and you cannot say: "This is the symbol of a flame," because you will die of the heat of this flame. So is Christ not a symbol for something. It is the substance in itself. It means life. It means power, the power of life. It brought already life. Without this substance of Christ the earth would already have died. So it's not a symbol of something.

WIJERS: I thought, maybe his early death on the cross . . .

BEUYS: The cross is another thing. One could take the cross perhaps as a signature, or maybe as a symbol for earth. Because the cross would mean the materialistic constellation. The vertical and the horizontal line of the construction of the cube, and this is exactly the crystallized condition of death. So it is the exact, the proper transformation in a kind of letter, what the fate of earth from the beginning of the impulse of Christ towards our times means. The whole thing is nailed on this crystal-structure, of which every modern skyscraper is built; the whole building system, and the whole analytic system have to do with this orientating, basic mathematics. It has a lot to do with analytical mathematics.

I fear only always this declaration of symbols. Normally I do not work with symbols. But in translating the powers to a kind of image, or to a kind of writing, we have to use signs, or we have to use letters. And so this cross is a kind of letter to make clear what is going on. It shows the people an information on powers, if the people can read out of such a form, what such a form means.

But, you know, this is the dilemma in the whole reception of the art, that normally the people cannot read what this means, what a constellation of such lines would mean. They say: "Yes, it is a cross," you know, but . . . or: "It is a plus," or "It is two lines." That is the thing we have to educate, or we have to go in contact with, or we have to speak about. So we have, in fact, to create the language, because also the language is already dead. The languages are overflooded with elements of decay, you know. So bring out the new spirit in language and transport by the language the possibilities of humankind for its own development, that is the task we have to deal with.

But this is only possible if the people are looking at the phenomena without prejudice. And there is the barrier. Bring the people near to a kind of methodology where they learn to look at the phenomena without prejudice, because everybody looks with a kind of prejudice. Because he thinks he already knows about the powers and how the powers have their links, or have their interdependency. And that is the dilemma; that they cannot look without prejudice, which is implanted by a very, very restrictive education during the last two hundred years: in schools, universities, in the media, in the idea of science with this one-sidedness which gave the people such a kind of prejudice, and this understanding of life which is in reality a debasement of the idea of man. And because it is so debasing, it debased people. And in this debased existence one can only think after egoistic instincts, and think on living-standard and things that the materialistic system has developed.

And the materialistic system and the ruling powers in the world are interested to debase the ability of the people in the direction of such instincts as only to exploit, to live with this simple biological understanding of their machinery, that they look at their own life like they look at a car. The car needs fuel, and they think they need fuel, too. And the more food they can take, the more they take. And they take it away from other people. So it is a robbery, a general robbery and exploitation. That is the consequence of such an understanding of the world. And it is no wonder that this goes on, because the working places, the whole enterprise for the production of these ability-goods is in the hands of the states and the capitalistic, economical rulings of the things.

So the first thing we have to do: we have to liberate educating places, the cultural institutions, from the ruling and from the possession of the state and the economics.

WIJERS: But already many young people are going through this process on their own initiative.

BEUYS: That is true, yes. That is a very hopeful thing. So it is a hopeful thing that many young people are already born with another understanding of humankind's dignity and the values of humankind's life and spirit.

WIJERS: Nature does the work.

BEUYS: Yes. But sometimes the danger is to go then the private way, to go out of the connected responsibilities. Very often one finds a kind of tendency to privacy and that they go past the problems—go through and then they have nothing to do with the problem anymore.

WIJERS: For the work one needs people who feel they have a practical task to fulfill in this world.

BEUYS: We need the strongest of the spirits, who are able to resist in the middle of the shit, in the middle of the things, and who feel that their own ability can only grow in the middle of the problems and not in a kind of weak environment with a kind of spiritual feeling.

WIJERS: You mean: only in the battlefield one receives the real teachings.

BEUYS: Exactly.

WIJERS: Going to another question now. I wanted to ask you about Rudolf Steiner. It goes maybe a little bit away from . . .

BEUYS: No. It goes not away. It goes very practically in the middle of the center of the things. Because when we spoke about the possibilities in using Oriental spiritual values or the possibility for Christianity, I think, Rudolf Steiner was a person who followed the line along the possibilities, the creative possibilities, of Christianity in the Western world. He especially avoided to say that the spirit lies in the Eastern values of the mind. He saw surely that there exist a lot of spiritual possibilities in the East, but he did stress the necessity to bring it through the materialistic understanding of the world up to life. He did not avoid the Christian impulse of death.

So he did not avoid working with the materialistic understanding of the world. So he stood in the middle of the problems. And because he develops the things out of the middle of the destruction, and gave the examples, already then in comparison, for instance, with the Marxist ideas. He saw the problem very clearly. And also his social proposals, the so-called "Threefold Social Order," were very positive and were the only alternative in 1918, 1919, 1920, 1921. But the people did not understand, the people did not follow, because the materialistic impulse had a kind of priority to get through. By starting and breeding his power over already existing impulses in the German Romantic idealistic period . . .

WIJERS: Goethe . . .

BEUYS: Goethe, Hegel, Novalis, and Friedrich von Schiller were overruled by the materialistic understanding of the world, Steiner was on the line of the red thread. He had the line in his head and he showed already the kind of direction people should go, or would have to go. So therefore the whole historical analysis is very important to bring proposals for the solution of the problems

towards the future. And so there is not in discussion any inven-
tion in a kind of personal—what we in Germany call
"Liebhaberei" (hobby). No, there is a line of development in
history. And therefore such a personality like Rudolf Steiner is
very important to be mentioned, to explain the context.

WIJERS: When did you first come in contact with Rudolf Steiner's
writings?

BEUYS: The first contact I had with Steiner was during the war,
when I was a soldier. I read some books, but then I was not very
enthusiastic about the books. But I had some ideas in my mind
and then, when I came out of the war, I took again some lecture
and I found that this is a very, very important thing to be
discussed. And then I was in permanent contact with other
people who were working in this field of the Threefold Social
Order. And when I established in 1967 the Organization of the
Direct Democracy, it had at the same time the name: The
Threefold Social Order.

But surely also this constellation of proposals Steiner did in the
beginning of the Twenties, which did not succeed, which were
not taken over by the people, which were not understood—they
are more and more understood today. And they are also in a
better shape today, with better, one could say, with better inner
courage to show people the solution for the problems.

WIJERS: Did you add to his ideas something of your own?

BEUYS: I think, what I had to add to these things was a real other
thing, which has perhaps, in a way, nothing to do with Rudolf
Steiner, and this is the enlarged understanding of art. So it is a
constellation of methodologies, which I can work best with. But it

fits in a way. It fits with his idea of Threefold Social Order. It has an organic nearness to his ideas.

WIJERS: On art Rudolf Steiner writes that the artist has to bring divinity to the world.

BEUYS: But that is a kind of declaration every artist said already. Other things are better statements. Let me think if I have maybe only one better example. In German it would sound: *Die Wahrnehmung der Idee in der Wirklichkeit* (the reception of the idea in reality is the true communion of humankind). This is the meaning of the whole concept we were already speaking about, that the people in present times are not able to look towards the phenomena. They do not look towards the phenomena in such a way that they can read out of the phenomena the need of the phenomena and the idea of the phenomena. They come with a kind of materialistic prejudice and put it on the things. And so they made a distortion of reality, you know. They take only our one methodology and they take only the death-aspect of the phenomena.

And Steiner says: "The reception of the idea"—of the idea, this means the spiritual wholeness of the thing . . . "The reception of the idea in the phenomena is the communion of humankind with the spirit, with the truth." That is a more important thing of Steiner. And I think, what I try to develop sometimes, without consideration of any Steinerian impulse, is existing in the totality of art, and in the enlarged anthropological understanding of art. So the Social Sculpture fits in exactly in this understanding. But I, from my point of view, I see no other, and no better possibility in the present time, than to work with the idea of art, as the idea of creativity. And then this creativity means even the capital of the people, so it is linked to an economical idea. And this fits fantastically into the view some scholars of Rudolf Steiner developed in the last years. For instance economists who were thinking on the idea of the Threefold Society, like Wilhelm Schmundt. This fits exactly. And it is only natural that I am very friendly in discussion with Wilhelm Schmundt.

So that is therefore a very important element. But again the people try to bring up misunderstandings. Because even here in Germany there are some people only interested to shift away, only interested to go in contact with it again by those prejudices. And even very famous critics, they are only speaking like: "There is a kind of anthroposophical blah, blah in it," or they are speaking about a kind of "mysticism", because I mention the importance of Steiner. They are speaking about: "Anthroposophical oracles," you know. Here is a very, very, very other thing, the cultural distortion is very, very bad in some official writers, you know, who are very, very famous.

WIJERS: They have no idea of the origin of things.

BEUYS: No. And they have not even information on what was going on from the times of the Students Movement in Germany, or the May in Paris, or what the whole work was in the Organization of Direct Democracy, or the citizens initiatives. They are very far away in this *Nichtexistenz* (non-existence) of so-called modern art, but they feel capable and competent to speak about an enlarged understanding of art. So they are only laughing about the idea of the Social Sculpture, you know. That is the constellation, and this is better in the United States. They are more open and they are discussing these things.

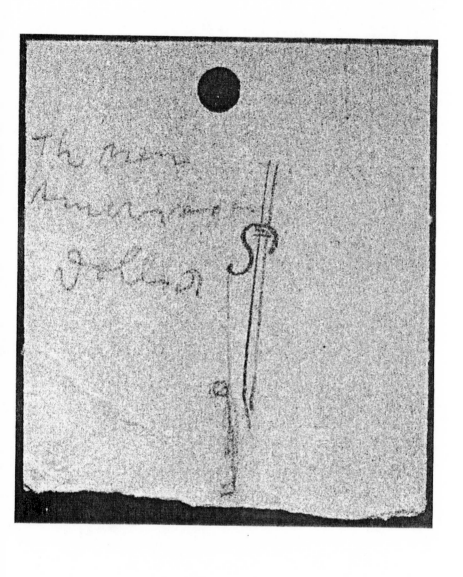

"LIFE COURSE / WORK COURSE"

("Lebenslauf/Werklauf") 1979

1921 Kleve Exhibition of a wound drawn together with plaster
1922 Exhibition of dairy cows Molkerei near Kleve
1923 Exhibition of a moustache cup (contents: coffee with egg)
1924 Kleve Open exhibition of heathen children
1925 Kleve Documentation: 'Beuys as Exhibitor'
1926 Kleve Exhibition of a stagleader
1927 Kleve Exhibition of radiation
1928 Kleve First exhibition of an excavated trench
     Kleve Exhibition to elucidate the difference between loamy sand and sandy loam
1929 Exhibition at the grave of Genghis Khan
1930 Donsbruggen Exhibition of heathers with healing herbs
1931 Kleve Connecting exhibition
     Kleve Exhibition of connections
1933 Kleve Underground exhibition (digging beneath the ground parallel to the surface)
1940 Posen Exhibition of an arsenal (together with Heinz Sielmann, Hermann Ulrich Asemissen and Eduard Spranger)

Exhibition of an airfield, Erfurt-Bindersleben
Exhibition of an airfield, Erfurt-Nord

1942   Sebastopol Exhibition of my friend
       Sebastopol Exhibition during the interception of a
       Ju-87

1943   Oranienburg Interim exhibition (together with Fritz
       Rolf Rothenburg + Heinz Sielmann)

1945   Kleve Exhibition of cold

1946   Kleve warm exhibition
       Kleve Artists' Union 'Profile of the Successor'
       Happening Central Station, Heilbronn

1947   Kleve Artists' Union 'Profile of the Successor'
       Kleve Exhibition for the hard of hearing

1948   Kleve Artists' Union 'Profile of the Successor'
       Düsseldorf Exhibition in the Pillen Bettenhaus
       Krefeld Exhibition 'Kullhaus" (together with A. R.
       Lynen)

1949   Heerdt Total exhibition three times in a row
       Kleve Artists' Union 'Profile of the Successor'

1950   Beuys reads 'Finnegans Wake' in 'Haus Wylermeer'
       Kranenburg Haus van der Grinten
       'Giocondologie'
       Kleve Artists' Union 'Profile of the Successor'

1951   Kranenburg 'Van der Grinten Collection' Beuys:
       Sculpture and Drawing

1952   Düsseldorf 19th prize in 'Steel and Pig's Trotter'
       (consolation prize, a light-ballet by Piene)
       Wuppertal Museum of Art Beuys: Crucifixes
       Amsterdam Exhibition in honour of the
       Amsterdam-Rhine Canal
       Nijmegen Museum of Art Beuys: Sculpture

1953 Kranenburg 'Van der Grinten Collection' Beuys: Painting

1955 End of the Artists' Union 'Profile of the Successor'

1956-57 Beuys works in the fields

1957-60 Recovery from working in the fields

1961 Beuys is appointed Professor of Sculpture at the Düsseldorf Academy of Art

Beuys adds two chapters to 'Ulysses' at James Joyce's request

1962 Beuys: The Earth Piano

1963 FLUXUS Düsseldorf Academy of Art

On a warm July evening on the occasion of a lecture by Allan Kaprow in the Zwirner Gallery, Cologne

Kolumba churchyard Beuys exhibits his warm fat Joseph Beuys Fluxus stable exhibition in Haus van der Grinten Kranenburg Lower Rhine

1964 documenta 3 Sculpture Drawing

1964 Beuys recommends that the Berlin Wall be heightened by 5 cm (better proportions!); 1964 Beuys VEHICLE ART; Beuys the Art Pill; Aachen; Copenhagen Festival; Beuys Felt works and Fat Corners. WHY?; Friendship with Bob Morris and Yvonne Rainer; Beuys: Mouse Tooth Happening Düsseldorf-New York; Beuys Berlin 'The Chief'; Beuys: The Silence of Marcel Duchamp is overrated. 1964 Beuys Brown Rooms; Beuys Stag Hunt (behind); 1965 and in us . . . under us . . . landunder; Parnass Gallery Wuppertal; Western Man Project; Schmela Gallery Düsseldorf: . . . any old noose . . ; Schmela Gallery Düsseldorf 'How to

Explain Pictures to a Dead Hare'; 1966 and here
already is the end of Beuys: Per Kirkeby '2.15';
Beuys Eurasia 32nd Set 1963—René Block, Berlin—
. . . with brown cross', Copenhagen: Traekvogn
Eurasia: Affirmation: the greatest contemporary
composer is the thalidomide child; Division of the
Cross; Homogen for grand piano (Felt); Homogen
for Cello (Felt); Manresa with Björn Nörregaard,
Schmela Gallery, Düsseldorf; Beuys The Moving
Insulator; Beuys The difference between Image
Head and Mover Head; Drawings, St. Stephan
Gallery, Vienna; 1967 Darmstadt Joseph Beuys and
Henning Christiansen: 'Hauptstrom'; Darmstadt Fat
Room, Franz Dahlem Gallery, Aha-Strasse, Vienna
Beuys and Christiansen: 'Eurasienstab' 82 minute
fluxorum organum; Düsseldorf June 21st, Beuys
founds the DSP German Student Party; 1967
Mönchengladbach (Johannes Cladders) Parallel
Process 1; Karl Ströher; THE EARTH TELEPHONE;
Antwerp Wide White Space Gallery: Image Head—
Mover Head (Eurasienstab); Parallel Process 2; THE
GREAT GENERATOR 1968 Eindhoven Stedelijk van
Abbemuseum Jan Leering. Parallel Process 3; Kassel
documenta 4 Parallel Process 4; Munich Neue
Pinakothek: Hamburg ALMENDE (Art Union);
Nuremberg ROOM 563 × 491 × 573 (Fat); Earjom
Stuttgart, Karlsruhe, Braunschweig, Würm-Glacial
(Parallel Process 5); Frankfurt: Felt TV II The Leg
of Rochus Kowallek not carried out in fat (JOM)!
Düsseldorf Felt TV III Parallel Process; Intermedia
Gallery Cologne: VACUUM—MASS (Fat) Parallel

Process, . . . Gulo borealis . . . for Bazon Brock;
Johannes Stüttgen FLUXUS ZONE WEST Parallel
Process—Düsseldorf, Academy of Art,
Eiskellerstrasse 1: LEBERVERBOT, Intermedia Gallery,
Cologne: Drawings 1947–1956; Christmas 1968:
Crossing over of the IMAGE HEAD track with the
track of the MOVER HEAD in All (Space) Parallel
Process—1969 Düsseldorf Schmela Gallery FOND III;
12.2.69 Appearance of MOVER HEAD over the
Düsseldorf Academy of Art; Beuys takes the blame
for the snowfall from 15th–20th February; Berlin—
René Block Gallery: Joseph Beuys and Henning
Christiansen Concert: I attempt to set (make) you
free—Grand piano jom (zone jom). Berlin: National
Gallery; Berlin: Academy of Art: Sauerkraut Score—
Eat the Score! Mönchengladbach: Transformation
Concert with Henning Christiansen; Düsseldorf
Kunsthalle Exhibition (Karl Ströher); Lucerne Fat
Room (Clock); Basel Kunstmuseum Drawings;
Düsseldorf PROSPECT: ELASTIC FOOT PLASTIC FOOT

1973 Joseph Beuys born in Brixton

CONTRIBUTORS

BERNHARD JOHANNES BLUME An artist based in Cologne, he has collaborated with Anna Blume on photographic theater pieces. In the Sixties he participated at several Fluxus events in Düsseldorf with and by Joseph Beuys, under whom he studied at the Staatliche Kunstakademie Düsseldorf. In 1981, he and Joseph Beuys gave a talk about trees under the motto "pure ratio is green."

ACHILLE BONITO OLIVA Italian art critic who became prominent as the expert of the Italian Transavanguardia, the group of figurative painters including Enzo Cucchi, Sandro Chia, Mimmo Paladino, Francesco Clemente and others that surged in the late Seventies, early Eighties. He has widely published on Futurism, Marcel Duchamp, Paul Klee, *arte povera,* minimal art and Joseph Beuys.

EDIT deAK A film-maker and art critic who has contributed to publications such as *Artforum, Art in America* and others. She is the co-publisher and editor of *Art-rite* magazine.

RICHARD DEMARCO An Italo-Scot born and bred in Edinburgh. Presenter of 260 theater productions and over 2000 visual art events, he introduced into Great Britain the avant-garde of West Germany, Austria, Poland, Romania, Yugoslavia, Italy, France in the Sixties, Seventies and Eighties and was the first gallery director to present the art of Joseph Beuys in the English-speaking world.

KATE HORSEFIELD   Art critic and video artist, co-founder of the Video Data Bank, the largest distributor of artists' videos in the United States. She is the co-producer of the videotapes "Ana Mendieta: Fuego de Tierra" and "Video Against AIDS."

CARIN KUONI   Born in Switzerland, a free-lance art critic based in New York. She has written for publications such as *artis*, *Kunst-Bulletin* and the *Neue Zürcher Zeitung*.

KIM LEVIN   Art critic for the *Village Voice*, author of *Beyond Modernism; Essays on Art from the Seventies and Eighties* (Harper and Row, 1988).

ALAN MOORE   Born in Chicago in 1951, a writer and video producer living in New York. He is a co-founder of ABC No Rio. The "Real Estate Show" which he organized there in 1980 was a landmark in New York's alternative art scene, protesting gentrification of artists' neighborhoods. It was closed by police force, despite rallies in its support at which Joseph Beuys participated.

ART PAPIER   An art handler at the Guggenheim Museum during the installation of the Joseph Beuys retrospective in 1979, he is now a biology researcher at Columbia University.

WILLOUGHBY SHARP   A video artist and the director of the Willoughby Sharp Gallery in New York. He worked at the Guggenheim Museum and the Museum of Modern Art in New York where he was co-organizer of the "Information Show" in 1970.

He is co-founder of *Avalanche* magazine and is a teacher at the School of Visual Arts in New York City.

CAROLINE TISDALL   Born in 1945 in Stratford-upon-Avon, she is a writer, art historian and film maker. She is the author of many books, including *Futurism* (Thames & Hudson, 1977) *Beirut, Frontline Story* (Pluto, 1983) and *Witches' Point* (Demarco, 1987). She wrote several books on Joseph Beuys and curated many exhibitions. Her books on Beuys include *The Secret Block for a Secret Person in Ireland* (Oxford, 1974), *Coyote* (Schirmer-Mosel, 1976), and *Joseph Beuys* (Guggenheim Museum/Thames & Hudson, 1979).

LOUWRIEN WIJERS   An art critic and writer based in Amsterdam, she arranged for the meeting between the Dalai Lama and Joseph Beuys in 1982, which, however, was not recorded. She is the organizer of the symposium "Art meets Science and Spirituality in a changing Economy" in Amsterdam (1990).

SOURCES OF TEXTS

Unless otherwise noted, the original language is English.

I SOCIAL SCULPTURE

"Introduction" (1979), in: Caroline Tisdall, *Joseph Beuys*. Exhibition catalog, The Solomon R. Guggenheim Museum, New York City, New York (Thames and Hudson), 1979, p. 7

"I am searching for field character" (1973), in: *Art into Society, Society into Art*. Exhibition catalog, The Institute of Contemporary Arts, London. London (ICA), 1974, p. 48, translation (according to supplement sheet): Norman Rosenthal, Martin Scutt, or Caroline Tisdall

A public dialogue. New York City, The New School for Social Research, January 11, 1974 in: *Avalanche Newspaper* (New York), May 1974, p. 5ff. [available as 120 minutes VHS tape from the Willoughby Sharp Gallery, 8 Spring Street, New York City 10012]

"I put me on this train!", interview with Art Papier, New York City, The Solomon R. Guggenheim Museum, November 2, 1979, in: *Wedge* (New York), vol. 1, no. 1, 1980, p. 5ff.

Speech upon receiving an honorary doctorate degree from the Nova Scotia College of Art and Design, Halifax, May 8, 1976, in: *Parachute* (Montreal), vol. 1, no. 4, fall 1976, p. 23

II ITS ELEMENTS

Interview with Kate Horsefield, New York City, The Solomon R. Guggenheim Museum, January 1980, in: *Profile* (Video Data Bank, Chicago), vol. 1, no. 1, January 1981, p. 5ff. Transcript of a video by Lyn Blumenthal and Kate Horsefield, produced by Video Data Bank

Interview with Willoughby Sharp, Düsseldorf, the artist's studio, August 28, 1969, in: *Artforum* © *Artforum* (New York), December 1969, p. 40 ff. translation: Marianne Landré

"Time's Thermic Machine", a public dialogue. Joseph Beuys in conversation with Bernhard Johannes Blume and the audience at Galerie Magers, Bonn, April 24, 1982, in: Bonito Oliva, Achille and Alanna Heiss, Kaspar König (Ed.), *Quartetto*, Milano (Arnoldo Mondadori Editore), 1984, p. 105–109, translator unknown

Interview with Richard Demarco, London, March 1982, in: *Studio International* (London), vol. 195, no. 996, September 1982, p. 46f.

Discussions of a few objects and an action piece with Caroline Tisdall, spring 1974 and fall 1978, excerpts from: Caroline Tisdall, *Joseph Beuys*. Exhibition catalog, The Solomon R. Guggenheim Museum, New York City, New York (Thames and Hudson), 1979; and: Caroline Tisdall, Joseph Beuys, *Coyote*, Munich (Schirmer-Mosel), 1980 (2nd edition) partially translated by Caroline Tisdall

Joseph Beuys and Heinrich Böll, "Manifesto for a Free International University," 1973, in: *Art into Society, Society into Art*. Exhibition catalog, The Institute of Contemporary Arts, London. London (ICA), 1974, p. 49ff.

"Death keeps me awake", interview with Achille Bonito Oliva, Rome, 1973, in: Armin Zweite (Ed.), *Joseph Beuys zu Ehren*, Exhibition catalog, Städtische Galerie im Lenbachhaus, Munich. Munich (Städtische Galerie im Lenbachhaus), 1986, p. 606ff.

III THE SITE

Joseph Beuys and the Dalai Lama.
Joseph Beuys, interview with Louwrien Wijers, Düsseldorf, the artist's studio, November 4, 1981 in: press release, n.d. (archives of Ronald Feldman Fine Arts, New York City)
Conversation between Lama Sogyal Rinpoché and Joseph Beuys, Paris, January 29, 1982, in: Louwrien Wijers, *Embracement of East and West*. Velp (Kantoor voor Cultuur Extracten), June 1982, p. 81ff.

Interview with Alan Moore and Edit deAk, New York City, René Block Gallery, January 1974, in: *Some artists, for example Joseph Beuys*. Multiples, Drawings, Videotapes. Exhibition catalog. The University of California (The University Art Gallery), Riverside, 1974, n.p. © 1974 Regents of the University of California

Interview with Louwrien Wijers, Düsseldorf, the artist's studio, November 22, 1979, in: *Joseph Beuys talks to Louwrien Wijers*, Velp (Kantoor voor Cultuur Extracten), 1980, n.p.

"Life Course/Work Course" ("Lebenslauf/Werklauf"), 1979, in: Caroline Tisdall, *Joseph Beuys*. Exhibition catalog, The Solomon R. Guggenheim Museum, New York City, 1979, New York (Thames and Hudson), 1979, p. 9

PHOTOGRAPHIC CREDITS

FRONT COVER: Joseph Beuys, "Coyote, I Like America and America Likes Me." René Block Gallery, New York City, 1974 © Caroline Tisdall, 1974

BACK COVER: Joseph Beuys signing his multiple "Noiseless Blackboard Eraser", 1974, at the Ronald Feldman Fine Arts, New York City, 1974. Photograph by Klaus Staeck and Gerhard Steidl. © Edition Staeck, 1974

FRONTISPIECE: Joseph Beuys, "The Invincible" ("*der Unbesiegbare*"), 1963 © Eva Beuys-Wurmbach, 1963

PAGE 108: Extension of the action "7000 Oaks" ("7000 *Eichen*"), conceived for documenta 7, Kassel, 1982 and completed 1987. Its first American site in front of the Dia Art Foundation exhibition space in New York City, 1988. © Carin Kuoni, 1990

PAGE 118: Joseph Beuys, "Rubberized Box" ("*Gummierte Kiste*"), 1957. The Ströher Collection, Hessisches Landesmuseum, Darmstadt, West Germany. © Hessisches Landesmuseum Darmstadt, 1990

PAGE 122: Joseph Beuys, "Lavender Filter" ("*Lavendelfilter*"), 1961. The Lone Star Foundation Inc. Collection, New York. © Galerie Karsten Greve, Cologne, 1990

PAGE 124: Joseph Beuys, "Fat Chair" (*"Stuhl mit Fett"*), 1963. The Ströher Collection, Hessisches Landesmuseum, Darmstadt, West Germany. © Eva Beuys-Wurmbach, 1990

PAGE 130: Joseph Beuys, "The Pack" (*"das Rudel"*), 1969. The Ströher Collection, Hessisches Landesmuseum, Darmstadt, West Germany. © Hessisches Landesmuseum Darmstadt

PAGE 132-140: Joseph Beuys, "Coyote, I Like America and America Likes Me." One week performance at the occasion of the opening of the René Block Gallery, New York City, May 1974. © Caroline Tisdall, 1974

PAGE 146: Joseph Beuys, "Fond III/3," 1979 (foreground), "Brazilian Fond," 1979 (background). Collection, The Dia Art Foundation, New York. © Dia Art Foundation, Jon Abbott, 1974

PAGE 259: Joseph Beuys, "The New American Dollar," 1974. Collection Caroline Tisdall. © Caroline Tisdall, 1989 *from Four Walls Eight Windows:*

JEAN DUBUFFET
Asphyxiating Culture and Other Writings
INTRODUCTION BY THOMAS M. MESSER
ISBN: 0-941423-09-3
cloth/$17.95

274